PRAISE FOR
Secrets Savored

"Most of my life I've been the beneficiary of godly women that the Lord placed along my path. Not having a mother from the age of 10 left me without a role model. But, God in his loving grace, sent women to teach, guide, and love me. Because of their profound influence on my life, I desire to minister to young women. Secrets is an avenue God has provided for me. What a joy it is to me as God directs my path with the young women He has given me."

Karen Looney Jett
Discipling Leader

"When my husband and I moved to a new city, not knowing anyone, Secrets Savored gave me the opportunity to connect with other women also seeking to grow closer to Jesus and discover His purpose for our lives. This ministry brings together women of all ages, backgrounds, and stages of life in such a sweet way that has blessed me."

Sarah Sherlock
Secrets Savored Participant

"Before I knew about Secrets Savored, I prayed that God would allow me to learn from godly women as it says in Titus 2. I am so grateful that He answered my prayers. I have learned so much from the discipling leaders about God's Word and how to be a godly wife and homemaker. I have also learned to follow Christ through the example of the leadership. I cannot thank you enough for showing me how to love Christ supremely and to love my husband."

Jenny McKay
Secrets Savored Participant and Pastor's Wife

"The most important ministry a Christian can have is discipleship, and Secrets Savored is an excellent tool in carrying out that Biblical mandate. In a warm and inviting home setting, young women are led to discover and practice godly living. I have enjoyed being a discipler in a program that balances both the practical and spiritual needs of women. As we talk, eat, study, and have fun together, we develop strong bonds that will last a lifetime. What a blessing!"

Elisa Skinner
Discipling Leader

SECRETS *Savored*

Creating Community Through Simple Hospitality

Book Two

DIANNE DOUGHARTY

Workbook

HIGH BRIDGE BOOKS
HOUSTON

SECRETS SAVORED
Book Two Workbook

Copyright © 2023 by Dianne Lynn Dougharty
All rights reserved.

No part of this publication may be reproduced, stored in a retrieval system, or transmitted in any form or by any means electronic, mechanical, photocopying, recording, or otherwise, without the prior written permission of the author.

Scripture quotes are taken from New Living Translation Second Edition, Tyndale House Publishing Company, Carol Stream, Illinois, Copyright ©1968, 1989, 1990, 1991, 1993, 1996, 2004 by Tyndale House Publishing Incorporated. New King James Version, Copyright 1982 by Thomas Nelson, Inc.

New American Standard Bible: Ryrie Study Bible, ©1986, 1995 by The Moody Bible Institute. The New Living Translation Parallel Study Bible, ©2011 by Tyndale House Publishers. The NIV/Message Parallel Bible Copyright © 2004 The Zondervan Corporation, Grand Rapids, Michigan 49530.

Library of Congress Control Number: 2012945608
ISBN: 978-1-954943-11-7

Graphic Design by *Studio B Print and Design*, Tyler Bedwell

Cover Photography: Jo Laura Bell Photography

Printed in the United States of America U.S. Printing History

First Edition: August 2012

Requests for Information should be addressed to:

Secrets Savored, Inc.
P.O. Box 2257
Cordova, Tennessee 38088

High Bridge Books
Houston, TX

For purchasing the Secrets Savored Book Two Leader Guide complete with weekly lesson plans or the Book Two Workbook for participants go to www.secretsavored.org/curriculum/shop.

You will need one Workbook per participant.

TO MY MOM, DR. BEVERLY CLECKNER
TO MY MOTHER-IN-LAW,
MRS. NELL DOUGHARTY

*Y*ou both impacted my life and gave me a deep desire to be the best wife, mom, and homemaker that I could be. Mom, you sacrificed so much to raise four children and complete your education in the process; always making sure we were well fed, clothed, and lovingly cared for. Your faithfulness, devotion, and commitment to the Lord, your husband, your family, and others have been an example to me. God has abundantly blessed me with being your daughter!

*M*y mother-in-law, Nell, treated me like a daughter from the day Mark brought me to Florida to meet his family. I am grateful for the beautiful example she set for me of a modern-day Naomi. Her love of family and home, as well as ministry, was a wonderful example to me. Her years of teaching and investing in young women as a teacher in the public school system was a gift to many. She is dearly missed!

"A gracious woman retains honor."
Proverbs 11:16a NKJV

"Strength and honor are her clothing; she shall rejoice in time to come.
She opens her mouth with wisdom, and on her tongue is the law of kindness.
She watches over the ways of her household, and does not eat the bread of idleness.
Her children rise up and call her blessed; her husband also, and he praises her."

Proverbs 31:25-28 NKJV

WITH GRATITUDE

I am afraid if I try to list the names of all those I owe gratitude, I would neglect someone. So, let me begin with the One without whom none of this would be possible, my heavenly Father. I am grateful to the Lord that He knows best. I would have never dreamed that out of life's most difficult hardship, this ministry would be birthed! Thank you, Father!

> "The Lord says, 'I will guide you along the best pathway for your life.
> I will advise you and watch over you.'"
>
> Psalm 32:8 NLT

To the many young women who participated in the Secrets ministry around the country these past several years, I love you! Thank you for letting us pour into your lives all the secrets we have attained over the years. I pray this study and the lives of the discipling leadership have profoundly impacted your life and home.

A word of gratitude goes to JoLaura Bell of JoLaura Bell Photography for our cover and Tyler Bedwell of Studio B Print & Design for designing our logo and formatting the books. I owe you girls a huge thank you for your service, incredible creativity, and patience!

To my friend and mentor, Marge, who now resides in heaven, I owe a debt of gratitude for her editing expertise and help. She was always one to go far beyond the "second mile" in order to help a friend.

To our board, thank you for your tireless work and commitment. My heartfelt appreciation goes to the Harry Smith Foundation for the funding to publish the original curriculum material; you were a direct answer to our prayers!

Thank you to those in the body of Christ who gave to Mark and me in so many ways over the years of his illness. You believed in this ministry and prayed for us as God led us down a dark road and through deep waters. Your continued support upon Mark's death has been a blessing to me. To my sweet sisters in Christ—thank you for your love, prayers, listening ears, timely hugs, girl moments, the supplied Kleenex, and the laughter, which at times along the journey were much needed and appreciated—I love you!

I want to thank my parents for their encouragement and belief over the years that I could do anything. I never doubted their love or support! To my siblings and Mark's family, I am grateful for your love, support, encouragement, prayers, and belief in God's calling upon my life. Last, but not least, I am very grateful to my daughters, Angela and Kelly, my sons-in-law, and grandchildren for their patience and sacrifice of time away from Mom and Mimi, while I was doing what God had called me to do. How grateful I am for you. You are treasured and loved a bunch!

CONTENTS

Weekly Recipes XI
Introduction to Secrets Savored XIII
Weekly Bible Study XV
Understanding the Bible XVI

WEEK ONE
Organizing Your Home 21

WEEK TWO
Organizing Your Closet 39

WEEK THREE
Tips on Laundry, Ironing, and Sewing 53

WEEK FOUR
Etiquette 71

WEEK FIVE
Etiquette for Children 91

OPTIONAL WEEK FIVE
Shower and Party Etiquette 109

WEEK SIX
Tips on Cleaning 129

WEEK SEVEN
Decorating Made Simple 153

WEEK EIGHT
Tips on Gardening, Flowers, and Canning 175

WEEK NINE
Woman to Woman 193

Time in the Kitchen Recipes 204
Secrets Savored Participation Sheet 217

Weekly Recipes

WEEK THREE | 54

Powdered Laundry Detergent
Liquid Laundry Detergent

OPTIONAL WEEK FIVE | 112

Wedding Shower Recipes:
Hope's Coffee Slush
Refreshing Punch
Baby Carrots with Herb Dressing
Pesto and Turkey Pinwheels
Bacon and Cheese Dip
Chocolate Hazelnut Dipped Strawberries
Mini Almond Cupcakes
Baby Shower Recipes:
Hope's Coffee Slush
Sorority House Casserole
Fruit Kabobs
Lemon Blueberry Mini Muffins
Party Recipes:
Cajun Grilled Beef Tenderloin
Oven-Roasted Squash
Roasted Rosemary Potatoes
Blueberry Pound Cake

WEEK SIX | 128

Homemade Spray Cleaner
Homemade Household Cleaner

WEEK EIGHT | 181

Peach Preserves
Heirloom Tomato Salsa
Olita's Sweet Pickles
Bread and Butter Pickles
Spaghetti Sauce
Chow Chow
Barbeque Sauce

TIME IN THE KITCHEN RECIPES | 204

Whole Wheat Yeast Rolls
Yeast Doughnuts
Whole Wheat Orange Muffins
Sour Cream Blueberry Muffins
Christine's Fabulous Coconut Smoothie
Peanut Butter Coconut Power Balls
Six-Ingredient Granola Bars
Whole Wheat Pita Chips
Cheesy Almond Dip
Pan-Seared Cod
Creamy Salmon Filets
Trout Amandine with Lemon Sauce
Sweet Cream Chocolate Cake
Creamy Chocolate Icing
Red Velvet Cupcakes
Cream Cheese Icing
Strawberry Filled Cupcakes
Sugar Cookies
Linda's Old Fashioned Sugar Cookie
Lemon Bars
Peppermint Ice Cream
Spiced Hot Cocoa

INTRODUCTION
to Secrets Savored

As a child, I attended church, but unfortunately, I grew up believing that I had to keep a certain set of rules in order to be a Christian. I was always breaking the rules; therefore, I never felt "good enough" or accepted by God.

My husband, Mark, grew up in the same church. Once we were married, we did what most people do who feel that they can never be acceptable to God—we ran from Him. The first few years, we ran hard after the world and away from God. Although our lives were full of things and stuff, we lacked meaning and purpose and peace and joy. We had much, yet we had nothing because we did not have Jesus Christ—who is everything.

> In Romans 11:6 it says, "And since it is through God's kindness, then it is not by their good works. For in that case, God's grace would not be what it really is—free and undeserved." NLT

God tells us that salvation does not come as a result of anything we do, nor because we deserve it, but because of His mercy and grace through the shed blood of His Son, Jesus. It is a free and undeserved gift.

> "For by grace you have been saved through faith. And this is not your own doing; it is a gift of God." Ephesians 2:8 ESV

God intervened in our lives after eleven years of marriage, and Mark was saved. As he studied God's Word, he began to see that it was not by our works or in keeping a set of rules that we are saved, but by the shed blood of Jesus. It was in his accepting Jesus as his personal Lord and Savior that his life was drastically changed. Just a few months after he was saved, I gave my heart and life to Jesus. Thus, my life was forever changed!

The relationship Mark and I had with Christ over the years *determined* the trajectory of our lives, marriage, and family. That relationship sustained me over the eleven years of journeying with him through a dreadful disease called Multiple Systems Atrophy. And, that relationship sustains me now as I adjust to living life without my soulmate and best friend.

In the midst of our journey, God led me to begin a mentoring ministry called Secrets Savored. This ministry is based on the verses in Titus 2 that encourage older women to teach younger women by giving them encouragement and strength for living out the life before them. Often, people ask me why the name Secrets Savored? What is the secret? Would you like to know the secret of Secrets Savored?

The ***secret*** of Secrets Savored is ***Jesus***!

In this fatherless, iPhone, Facebook, Twitter, and Instagram, self-driven world, Jesus is the only way to true peace and joy. He is the answer for discontentment, insecurity, depression, anxiety, and broken hearts. Secrets Savored is God's tool for reaching young women with the message of relationship versus rules. Through the lives and examples of older godly women and practical and biblical teaching, young women can grow to understand that there is no true peace, joy, contentment, or meaning in life apart from a personal relationship with *Jesus*. I want them to know they are valued by Him, and what they do in life for Him will count and reap a grand reward in the end.

> "Therefore, since we have been made right in God's sight by faith, we have peace with God because of what Jesus Christ our Lord has done for us." Romans 5:1 NLT

I am excited that you are joining this community of women who desire to create a spirit of hospitality and Christlikeness within your lives, homes, and relationships—for the glory of God!

Dianne

WEEKLY BIBLE STUDY

*The main purpose in studying the Bible is so that we will know God.
If we know the Bible, we will thus know the God of the Bible.*

The Bible ...

- **INFORMS US**
- **INSTRUCTS US**
- **GUIDES US**
- **CORRECTS AND CONVICTS US**

In Psalms 119:11 it says, "I have hidden your word in my heart that I might not sin against you"(NIV). If we hide scripture and biblical truths in our hearts, it will protect us, and we will always have a word of encouragement and instruction to draw upon.

Women are relational, and women relate to other women. God made us that way. Because of that, we will be studying women in the Bible. We will learn biblical principles from each of their lives for living that if followed and applied will protect us from harmful thoughts and actions. Example:

- In studying Sarah, Abraham's wife, we learn about the biblical principle of waiting on God, and the consequences of not being willing to wait on Him.

- In studying Rahab, we learn the biblical principle of obedience equals blessing. Her faith led her to trust that God would take care of her and her family. Because she trusted God. He blessed her by placing her in the lineage of Christ.

Many of the women we will be studying over the next few weeks made good choices, but then, others made bad choices. In life, we all make some good and some bad choices. In our study, we will see the blessings of good choices and the consequences of bad choices. God has placed each one within His story so that you and I might relate to them and learn from their lives.

In the workbook participants will find a question sheet to complete prior to class each week. The questions will relate to the passage of scripture read for that week's lesson. The study time required should not exceed thirty minutes.

We will only receive what we are willing to put into the devotional study each week. Remind the participants that hiding God's Word in our hearts means we will always have a word from Him for any circumstance we face. May each woman be blessed as a result of her obedience to study God's Word!

Understanding THE BIBLE

Each week, we will be studying women in the Bible. The Bible is a large book covering a lot of information and many topics. Let's get familiar with the books that are found in the Bible—66 in all!

BOOKS OF THE BIBLE:

Old Testament: An account of a Nation: Israel (Jewish people)

Genesis	2 Chronicles	Daniel
Exodus	Ezra	Hosea
Leviticus	Nehemiah	Joel
Numbers	Esther	Amos
Deuteronomy	Job	Obadiah
Joshua	Psalms	Jonah
Judges	Proverbs	Micah
Ruth	Ecclesiastes	Nahum
1 Samuel	Song of Solomon	Habakkuk
2 Samuel	Isaiah	Zephaniah
1 Kings	Jeremiah	Haggai
2 Kings	Lamentations	Zechariah
1 Chronicles	Ezekiel	Malachi

New Testament: An account of a Man: Jesus

Matthew	Ephesians	Hebrews
Mark	Philippians	James
Luke	Colossians	1 Peter
John	1 Thessalonians	2 Peter
Acts of the Apostles	2 Thessalonians	1 John
Romans	1 Timothy	2 John
1 Corinthians	2 Timothy	3 John
2 Corinthians	Titus	Jude
Galatians	Philemon	Revelation

Three Easy Steps for Studying the Bible...

As you read the Bible, consider these key steps, and you will gain a better knowledge of what you are reading:

STEP 1: Observation—What does the passage say?

- Look carefully at what it says and how it says it.

- Pay attention to the terms, words, etc. Words can have many meanings, but terms are words used in a specific way in a specific context.

- A paragraph is a complete unit of thought.

- The amount of space or the number of chapters or verses given to a specific topic will reveal the importance of that topic.

- *Repetition* is used to demonstrate that something is important. So, watch for repeated words or topics.

- Pay close attention, for example, to certain relationships that appear in the text.

- Be sure you notice the atmosphere, mood, tone, or urgency of the writing.

- *Ask* Who? Who are the people in this passage?
  Ask What? What is happening in this passage?
  Ask Where? Where is this story taking place?
  Ask When? When in time (of day, of the year, in history) is it taking place?

STEP 2: Interpretation—What does the passage mean?

- Ask yourself what is the author's main thought or idea.

- Consider the entire context, verses that come before and after the one you are reading.

- Purchase a good Study Bible and do a cross-reference—look at other scriptures in the Bible noted beside the one you are reading. These verses will help you understand the context of the verse being read. (Example: The NLT Parallel Study Bible or the Ryrie NAS Study Bible)

- The Bible was written long ago, so when you are trying to figure out what it is saying, you need to understand it from the writer's cultural context. In the front of each book of the Bible, you will find a page informing you of all the details related to that book: The time in which it was written, location, author, etc. Reading this page will give you a better knowledge of what you will be reading.

- Read commentaries by Bible scholars. These books can help you understand scripture. (Example: *Matthew Henry's Commentary on the Whole Bible*)

STEP 3: Application—What am I going to do about what the passage says and means?

- We study the Bible for the purpose of application. Applying what we have learned will change our lives. Obedience to God's Word will assist us in growing more like Jesus Christ.

- After we have observed a passage and interpreted it to the best of our ability, we must then apply its truth to our own life.

- Asking the following questions will help you to better apply what you have learned:
  How does the truth I have read affect my relationship with God?
  How does this truth affect my relationship with others?
  How does this truth affect me?
  How does this truth affect my response to the enemy, Satan?

- The key to applying what you have read is putting into practice what God has taught you in your study. You may not be able to daily, consciously apply everything you have learned in Bible study, but you can consciously apply *some* of what you have learned.

- God blesses our efforts to apply His truth to our lives. Through our application of those truths, we will be conformed into the image of Jesus Christ.

Week One

ORGANIZING YOUR HOME

Introduction

NOT NATURALLY *Organized*

*W*hat makes reorganizing and cleaning out drawers and cabinets synonymous with beginning a new year? Many of us have this incredible desire to create order in our lives when a new year arrives. The stores, Pinterest, and television commercials push the sales of plastic bins and new methods for organizing. But, what about the rest of the year? Wouldn't it be nice to have order year round?

Just the idea of organizing, whether a drawer or closet, can often be frustrating and overwhelming for those who are not naturally organized. I love organization. In fact, when trying to clean the house, I am easily distracted by a closet or drawer that needs to be re-organized—which is play to me while cleaning is work! Organization is one of many gifts or abilities God gives to people. To some He gives the gift of organization, to others the gift of encouragement, and to others the gift of leadership and on and on we could go. We were all created differently and with unique skill sets.

We were given different gifts and abilities, but there is one thing that God gave to every individual and that is TIME.

> "Time is really the only capital any human being has,
> and the one thing he can't afford to waste."
>
> Thomas Edison, American Inventor

*B*y using the word capital, Edison was saying that time is an asset or something of value. What do we do with time? We waste time, we spend time, we invest time, and we take time for granted. Being disorganized causes us to waste time. For example, time can be wasted by spending an hour looking for important papers that could have been found immediately if there had been a system in place. Before you know it, you've spent an hour looking for papers you cannot find. And that is just one hour in one day for one item—multiply that by a lifetime! How much time are you wasting each week, each month, and each year because you will not place organization as a priority? Time wasted is time lost—never to be regained!

Many people think they can succeed among the chaos of disorganization, but disorganization can cost a high price. It can cost a promotion at work, it can decrease your productivity and it can cause added stress and limit your effectiveness. Whether you have a natural gift of organization or not, you can learn to be more organized. And, when you are, your life will be much less stressful and more fulfilling. Remember, time is capital, and organization is a great way to invest in your capital!

We are so excited that you have chosen to be a part of this Secrets class! This study is designed to be fun, informative, and educational. You will love some of the subjects covered and others you will not love, but each is necessary for keeping a home and having a home that reflects Christ.

MESSIES CLASSIFIED [1]
Find yourself amidst these Messies ...

PERFECTIONIST MESSIE—Very high standards! Rest of house may be a wreck, but she decides to clean the oven and it is very, very well done; she's exhausted and can do no more!

REBELLIOUS MESSIE—Has psychological hang-ups from childhood. Mom insisted on cleanliness and order, and now that she is grown she is going to show independence by defiance!

RELAXED MESSIE—Rationalizes that the world outside is hostile and home is the place to relax. Why work at home too? So things are let go! Truth is that messiness is NOT relaxing. It causes strain, pressure, and jangled nerves!

SENTIMENTAL MESSIE—Every scrap of paper and every shell brought home by Johnny is precious! Old, undeveloped film and flash drives strewn in drawers! Stuff, stuff, stuff everywhere!

SPARTAN MESSIE—As ancient Spartans lived with only the necessities of life, this Messie believes that if there were less to care for, or if it were somehow shut up or nailed down and not used, it would be possible to handle it! Always looks for ways to eliminate "stuff."

CLEAN MESSIE—As long as things are CLEAN, they can be left out—clothes in basket not folded, dishes washed and left on counter. "But they are CLEAN, isn't that what counts?"

SAFE MESSIE—Leaves the bed unmade, "because it can air out better, and that kills more germs." Floors not waxed, "because they may be slippery and dangerous."

OLD-FASHIONED MESSIE—Loves doing things the old-fashioned way. The only good way is the old-fashioned way: clean the floor on hands and knees; bake pies and cakes from scratch; wax and buff the wooden floor with a cloth instead of a buffer; beat the rug instead of vacuuming it; use cloth instead of disposable diapers. Their motto is "Do it right, or not at all." A lot of time it turns out "not at all."

IDEALISTIC MESSIE—Head is usually in the clouds. Great thoughts and ideas are what interest this Messie. But the results are disastrous to an idealist. The beauty and charm, the satisfying family life, all melt under the heat of the messy home.

---

[1] Sandra Felton, *The Messies Manual* (Revell Publisher Grand Rapids, Michigan 2005).

ORGANIZATION

WHERE TO START

In Ecclesiastes 3:6b it says, "There is a time to keep and a time to throw away" (NAS). We often have good intentions of getting our homes and our lives in order, but it doesn't happen. I believe there are several reasons we never accomplish this:

- The task seems so overwhelming that we give up from the get-go
- We do not know where to start
- It is difficult to find the amount of time needed
- The task is so large that we lose motivation

Perhaps you, like so many of us, are trying to tackle too much. If you start with one drawer at a time, or one closet, and allow yourself twenty to forty minutes (more if job requires it) a week to accomplish your goal of getting that space uncluttered and organized, then maybe you wouldn't get overwhelmed or burned out and want to give up. Organization is something you learn. You learned to brush your teeth; you can learn this!

HOW TO GET STARTED

- Make a list of all the organizational projects you would like to accomplish this year; separate them by weeks and months.
- Take one area or room at a time, choosing the most often *lived-in* areas first. Be reasonable and patient. Things did not get into the condition they are in overnight.

If you were to decide to organize your kitchen in two hours, it would be the same as deciding to lose thirty pounds in the next four weeks. After your first week, you find that you have only lost one-half pound, so you become discouraged and give up. Make a list you can actually accomplish and learn to take advantage of small windows of time. For example, if you are on the phone catching up with a friend, clean out your jewelry case or drawer. When the children are eating lunch, choose one drawer in the kitchen to clean out. Look for pockets of time and maximize them. Do not sit for hours at your computer or on your iPhone; when you do, you are wasting valuable time. Respond to your emails and text messages and walk away. Choose wisely what you do with your time.

> "He (she) who tills his (her) land will have plenty of bread, but he (she) who pursues worthless things lacks wisdom." Proverbs 12:11 NKJV

> "In all labor there is profit, but mere talk leads only to poverty." Proverbs 14:23 NKJV

A PLACE *for Everything*

Benjamin Franklin said, "A place for everything, everything in its place." I don't believe Mr. Franklin realized that his words were the key to organizing your home. But, if everything has a place and is kept in its place, your home will be organized.

In the pages to come, I will help you simplify your organizational projects and provide shortcuts and systems, to save you time. Remember, time is capital!

FIVE BASIC RULES FOR BEGINNING
As mentioned before…

1. Take one room at a time. Tackling the entire house or apartment at once can be overwhelming.
2. As you approach the space, access the supplies needed to organize the room or space.
3. Purchase what is needed or find items that can be repurposed. Example: A woven basket that once held a floral arrangement can now be used to store gloves and scarves.
4. Once a room is organized, keep it that way. When that room is complete, move on.
5. If the space is really large, such as a master bedroom, children's playroom, or garage, divide the space, and take the time required to accomplish the task at hand.

An abundance of things can be one of the reasons the space you live in is unorganized. Let's start with a system to DECLUTTER…

1. Begin by preparing three bags, laundry baskets, or boxes labeled: Keep, Give-Away, and Throw Away.
   - When throwing away, a bag would make better sense.
   - When giving away, you could use a box which is easier to transport.
   - For all the items you keep, a laundry basket could be used to transport them to the location where they are normally stored.
2. Once your containers are in place and labeled, you are ready to organize your home or apartment one room at a time.
3. As you approach each item in a room, ask these questions:
   - Is this item necessary or vital to my livelihood?
   - Have I or anyone within my home used this item more than two times this year?

     Example: Things such as battery cables would be an exception, as you tend not to need them regularly, but they are a necessity. Use your discretion.

- How many of these do I have? Do I use all I have?

- Do I have sufficient room to store this item? Example: If an item cannot be conveniently stored in order to use it regularly, consider placing it in the give-away box.

Once these questions are answered, you will know what container to place the item into—the keep, throw away, or give-away.

> "There is a time to keep and a time to throw away."
> Ecclesiastes 3:6b NAS

ORGANIZATIONAL ADVICE FROM
The Happiness Project[2]
by Gretchen Rubin

Gretchen Rubin, author of the book *The Happiness Project*, was asked, "When there's so much that needs your attention—messy kitchen, messy desk, messy kids—what's the best place to start?" She said, 'Start with the thing that's making you crazy.' Think where your biggest boost would come from. The number one resolution that people mention to me as something that has made them happier is—to my surprise—making the bed. 'Over and over people who start doing it will say, Wow! It's a concrete thing you can do first thing in the morning. Then when you come back to bed, it's so much more inviting. Making your bed does not seem to be an important thing in a happy life, and yet it can be that tiny foothold into a more orderly life that sometimes people need.'"

When asked, "Why do these small changes, like making your bed, make such a difference?" "I think that the degree to which outer order contributes to inner calm is something that people really feel. Getting control of stuff makes people feel like they have more control over their lives—maybe irrationally, but it's one of these psychological truths."

In response to the interviewer's statement, "Let's talk about closets, the bane of so many of our lives." Gretchen responded, 'I always say you can self-medicate through closet cleaning. With closets, there's a decision that has to be made, and you just put off the decision. If you have never worn it, get rid of it. If you know you should not wear it, get rid of it. If it is hanging there with tags attached and you have never worn it, do not try to keep it to justify the expense of it, get rid of it.' When asked, "What is the best advice you've ever heard, she quoted, 'Put things away where you need to use them.'"

[2] Gretchin Rubin, "Organizational Advice from *The Happiness Project* (*Good Housekeeping Magazine*, January 2011).

ORGANIZING *Room by Room*

> "But all things must be done properly and in an orderly manner."
>
> 1 Corinthians 14:40 NAS

Even if you do not consider yourself orderly you can learn to have order beginning at the front door of your home. When others enter your home they can immediately sense if things are done in a proper and orderly manner. I am not saying that your home has to be immaculate or perfect, looking like a furniture showroom. There is nothing warm and inviting about that type of environment. But, order brings peace for those living in your home and for those visiting your home.

People "live" in homes. If you have roommates, pets, children, or a spouse, there is evidence that people "live" in your home from the front door to the back door—and that is okay. The key to restoring order is having a place for everything and everything in its place. When this is true, order can be restored quickly.

BEGIN AT THE FRONT DOOR

Typically, the front door area is where you welcome others into your home. You want to keep it as clutter-free as possible, making it easier for your guests to enter your home. When you have a closet filled with clutter at the front entrance, it can cause a major traffic jam when guests are attempting to get in the door and hang up coats. A clutter-free entryway closet and area makes it easier to welcome people into your home, and it can also help your guests to feel more at home.

ENTRYWAY

- A day or two before receiving guests, check the front closet to make sure there is no clutter.

- Clean out any excess items like seldom worn coats that can be stored in another closet or near the back door of the house where everyone exits on a daily basis.

- Keep the front closet for guests coats and items not used daily. Any items not hanging should be placed in a bin, basket, or container. Check to make sure you have plenty of extra hangers.

- To keep front door coat closets free of clutter, consider placing hooks and stackable units or baskets in the garage or in a mud room area for coats and items needed on a daily basis.

- If you do not have a front entry coat closet, direct your guests to where you would like for them to place their coats, purses, etc. Example: I direct our guests to the office where they may lay their things on one of two club chairs.

FAMILY ROOM

The family gathers in this room along with friends and guests. It is one of the most difficult rooms to keep clean and organized because it is constantly being utilized. Perhaps these tips will help you keep order in your family room.

- Look for ways to create storage space. Example: Ottoman with removable or hinged top, shelving on end tables, drawers and shelving on coffee table, bookcase, etc.

- When shopping for furniture, look for pieces that serve double-duty with more than one purpose. Example: Bench with storage underneath, sleeper sofa, etc.

- Utilizing a tray on the coffee table ensures a place for television remote controls, picture books, etc.

- Use large baskets to store magazines, throws, and books. Regularly go through these items. Discard or donate outdated magazines, toss or donate torn or used books, and give away additional throws. You can only read so many magazines and books. And, you only need one throw for each person living under your roof.

- For storing X-Box and Wii games, purchase a decorative box. Slide a label in each window on the front of decorative box in order to find your favorite game. Stackable drawers can also be used and stored in a cabinet, bookcase, or closet.

- Products such as Bongo Straps, Flexi Tie Cables, or a D-Line Zipper Cord are excellent for getting your extra electronic cords under control. Be sure to label the cords at the plug or strip so you will always know what goes with what! For keeping track of whose charging cord is whose, use different colored or patterned washi (duck) tape around each family members set of cords.

DINING ROOM

This room may seldom get used; therefore, it seldom needs your attention. Here are a few tips for keeping it orderly.

- My dining room is casual. I have a hutch with three open shelves on the top, three small drawers across the middle and an open shelf at the bottom. I needed a way to secure and organize the stacks of bowls, salad plates, etc., that were stored on the bottom of the hutch. I purchased old wire school locker baskets of various sizes to securely store the pieces of my pottery on the open bottom shelf.

- For the dinner plates, I purchased two round low-edged wire baskets and placed the dinner plates in one and the chargers in the other one on the main shelf.

- When I need plates or other pieces of my pottery, I just pull out a basket.

- The top open shelving is used to store/display the serving pieces and a few place settings.

- The drawers hold the nicer silverware and candles, etc., used in the dining room.

- All my glassware is stored in the kitchen. If you have a hutch with a closed cabinet and shelving, your stemware/glassware can be stored there. Keeping it all in one place ensures you will always be able to find it when needed.

- A sofa table serves well as a buffet, and a low chest can be used in the dining room for storage. I have a chest with drawers in the entry hall, right outside the dining room, in which I store placemats.

MASTER BEDROOM

We are often guilty of neglecting the private spaces in our homes. We decide that no one goes into our bedroom so it doesn't really matter whether it is clean and organized. It does matter because it is the room where you unwind, relax, and sleep.

Are you frustrated because your dresser drawers will not close? Consider cleaning them out. Take one drawer at a time, and as you remove items, ask yourself these four questions:

1. How long have I had this? Is it out of style?
2. Has it been longer than two years since I have worn it?
3. Is it a classic piece that will never go out of style?
4. Does it still fit? If not, can I replace it for less than the cost of alterations?

Based on the answers to the above questions, determine whether you should keep each item. If not, place in give-away or throw-away bags.

- Once all your dresser and/or chest of drawers are cleaned out, wipe out the drawers and place the clothes and items you are going to keep folded neatly inside.

- If closet space is limited, store out-of-season sweaters, skiwear, hats, gloves, etc., in plastic containers under the bed or on high shelving in the closet. Extra bedding for the master bedroom can be stored in the same manner.

- Remove coins, jewelry, and other small items from drawers. Use shoeboxes or small plastic boxes and trays to store these. Example: Cuff links, watches, pocket knives, etc.

- Discard all old or single socks.

- Throw away all stained garments.

- Cup hooks or plastic hooks can be used to hang jewelry, such as necklaces, on a wall in the closet. A bulletin board using pushpins is also a great way to organize jewelry.

- Keep only the necessary items, such as the book you are currently reading and a flashlight. Place smaller items in a drawer caddy or bin. Example: Pens, highlighters, nose spray, etc. All other non-essentials need to be cleaned out.

- In a walk-in closet, use baskets, bins, and wire cubes for extra storage.

- Collect the same type of hangers. Example: The felt covered non-slip hangers. This particular type of hanger will save space in your closet.

- Use a large decorative basket beside your bed or chair to store books, writing materials, throws, etc.

- If convenient, keep a laundry hamper in your closet or under the counter in your bathroom for collecting dirty clothes.

BATHROOM

A bathroom can be difficult to keep cleaned and organized because like the family room, it is continually in use. Below are tips that will help bring order to your bathrooms.

- In cabinets and linen closet, throw away old and partially full bottles of lotion, creams, nail polish, and sundry things. If you have not used the item in a year, chances are you will not use it again.

- Only keep items you use every day. Any makeup, moisturizers, or creams older than a year old should be thrown away. Bacteria can develop in these over time.

- Place hair styling care products, like curling iron, hair dryer, etc., in a stackable metal or plastic container.

- Consider plastic trays or bamboo divided trays for things such as tooth paste, tooth brushes, make-up, nail polish, tweezers, nail clippers, brushes, etc.

- Plastic or canvas boxes are good for storing products needed in personal hygiene. Example: Bottles of hairspray, extra shampoo and cream rinse, make-up bags, extra products such as soap and Q-tips, medicine, etc.

- Check expiration date on medicines, clean out those expired.

- First aid items can be stored in a snap-lid container.

- If linen closet does not exist or is small, towels can be rolled and placed in a large wicker basket beside the tub or outside of shower.

- If space allows, place two laundry baskets, one for darks and one for whites, in the master closet or linen closet.

- If you don't have a drawer space for make-up, store your make-up in a basket under the sink or in the linen closet.

- Basic cleaning products can be stored in a tub or bin under the sink.

LINEN CLOSET

Over the years, we collect linens. Some need to be kept, and others need to be cleaned out. If you have collected ten blankets thinking that one day your extended family may visit, and it has been fifteen years, and they still have not come, it may be time to give some of them away.

- Keep only the linens you can use and have room for. Place the remaining in the give-away container.

- If you have kept mis-matched sheets, that do not fit any mattress set in your home, place them in the give-away container.

- Once your final decisions are made as to what stays and what goes, wipe out the shelves and clean around the baseboards.

- Fold linens neatly on the shelves, arranging sheets and blankets according to size. If floor surface is available in linen closet, store extra items in a three-drawer unit on wheels.

- Towels and washcloths can be folded and stored in the linen closet or in the cabinets below the sink in the bathroom. Keep together all bath towels, hand towels, and washcloths, and stack according to size.

CHILDREN'S ROOMS

Teaching children to keep their rooms straight can be a daunting task; often it seems easier to do it yourself. But if that becomes the pattern, your children will never learn to be responsible and will become quite dependent on you—their maid! Get them involved in the following activities for organizing their room. Once their room is organized and straight, if old enough, they should be accountable in keeping it that way.

- Consider the function of the room and organize accordingly.

- In closet and drawers: Go through all the clothing every few months and make sure pieces still fit. Clean out any clothing that the child has outgrown or is worn out. Either give the clothing items away, save them for younger siblings, or if worn out, throw away.

- In the closet: Most poles are too high for children. Replace the existing pole with one no higher than four to six inches above your child's height. Poles should not exceed thirty-two inches in height. If you choose to leave the existing high pole, you can use it to store their out-of-season clothing.

- Purchase shelving that can be used for shoes, folded clothing, etc. Place the shelving horizontally at one end of the closet; having rods and shelves at their height makes it easier for them to put away their things.

- Utilize hooks inside doors, closets, and on walls. Hooks are a wonderful invention and easy for children. Use for robes, coats, etc. Label the hooks so the child knows what goes where. If the child is too young to read, use pictures or stickers to label hooks.

- A bookcase or wall unit works well for containers of small toys, puzzles, Barbie dolls, etc.

- Place similar items in plastic bins with lids. Example: Balls in one, all the puzzles in another, etc. Bins can also be made of canvas and wood but typically will not have a lid.

- Dirty Clothes: Place a hamper in your child's room and ask him to be responsible for placing his dirty clothes in the hamper. **For older children** (age seven and above): Find a divided hamper with a place for white and colored clothing. Labeled laundry baskets also work well. **For younger children** (ages 6 and below): They may need an incentive to pick up their dirty clothing. Consider putting an over-the-door or suction-mounted basketball goal above the laundry basket. Then the child can "dunk" his pjs into the basket.

- For school-age children, a desk is helpful for staying organized.

- Consider a hanging shoe bag for storing small items, shoes, socks, etc.

- Different colored laundry baskets or crates are great for storing toys. Purchase colors that coordinate with their room. These can often be stacked to save space.

- A basket for books. Having a basket designated for books will make their clean-up easier.

- Store all seasonal clothes in plastic tubs under the bed or in a storage area.

- Go through their toys every few months discarding the broken ones, giving away the seldom-used toys, and organizing the ones most often used. When discarding toys, it may be best to do it while the child is napping, at school, or distracted playing.

- If space is limited, consider buying plastic tubs with lids for storage. Rotate the toys every few months. It will be like Christmas when you bring out the toys that have been stored, and they will never miss the ones you chose to put away.

LAUNDRY ROOM

Between drops of dried detergent and softener and the lint from the dryer vent, a laundry room can be challenging to keep clean and organized. Each week when you clean your house, clean your laundry room as well. These tips may help you as you strive to keep your laundry room clean and orderly.

- Begin with removing all cleaners, soaps, and items in cabinets above the washer and dryer. Wipe cabinets clean. Place back only the items you use on a regular basis.

- Keep laundry soap, softener, dryer sheets, stain remover, and bleach at eye level close to the washer and dryer. If you are limited on space, a roller caddie is a great option.

- Place products in cabinet from left to right according to usage: stain remover, detergent, bleach, fabric softener, dryer sheets, spray-on starch, and bottle of water for steam iron.

- A folding surface is a necessity; if you are short on counter space, use the top of the washer or dryer. For hang-only clothing, use a dryer rack or an over the door hanger.

- If you have a hanging pole or additional space, keep extra hangers in the laundry room.

- Hanging clothes immediately after the drying cycle will save on ironing. Avoid allowing clothes to sit in a cold dryer or into a basket for days; they will end up crumpled.

- Use a plastic container for loose socks. Never let a single sock leave the laundry room. The chances of finding a mate at that point are minimal. If mate is not found, discard lone sock.

- The ironing board should be located near the iron, starch, and water bottle, preferably in the laundry room or whatever room you determine to be convenient for ironing.

- If space allows, laundry rooms are a good place for a bulletin board to hold all the school papers, announcements, the family calendar, etc. If space allows, place hooks on the wall for backpacks and coats and have a bin for shoes and boots.

Okay, I have given you some organizational advice and systems to put in place. It's time for you to get started. Remember, time is capital, strive for a place for everything and everything in its place!

The list of supplies and organizational containers that follow will help you get started in bringing order to your home.

WHAT'S NEEDED?

SUPPLIES AND ORGANIZATIONAL CONTAINERS...

1. Permanent marker to label containers: Keep, Give-a-Way, or Throw-Away.
2. Using clear large leaf bags will enable you to see what you have placed in the bag.
3. Boxes or laundry baskets can be used for separating items in cleaning out and reorganizing.
4. Drawer organizers: The number and size of each organizer will depend on the project.
5. Small plastic bins: Purchase ones with snap lids if storing small items that could spill out.
6. Small plastic containers: Example: Shoe box size.
7. Canvas, wood, or plastic boxes for storage.
8. Labels: White name tags or labels run from your computer can be used to label containers.
9. Bucket, water, rags, and cleaning products to clean as you reorganize.
10. Dusting products or *Swiffer* products, broom, dust pan, and/or *Dustbuster*.
11. Zipper-lock bags: These bags are great for storing buttons, safety pins, jewelry, etc.

BABY STEPS...

- Take one step at a time, one room at a time, and one day at a time.
- Be patient with yourself. Organizing a home or an apartment takes time.
- Make a list of goals or projects you would like to accomplish within your home and begin working down the list.
- Remember to enlist the help of others living in the home. You cannot do it alone—you will wear yourself out!
- Don't seek perfection for you or your home—offer yourself grace. Do the best you can in getting your place organized and keeping it that way, but realize a home is to be lived in and enjoyed.

MARY & MARTHA
Women with a Choice

Biblical Principle: As Christian women, we must choose to place God first if we desire to experience order and peace in our lives.

Read Luke 10:38–42

1. Martha welcomed Jesus into their home, but then "busied" herself. How did Mary respond to Jesus's visit?

2. What did Jesus say to Martha after she complained about her sister, Mary, not helping her?

3. Why was Martha's choice unwise?

4. What was it about Mary's choice that was wise?

5. How can making the choice to spend time with Jesus daily bring order into your life? Your home?

6. Our choices really do effect the way our lives and homes operate—with order and peace or chaos and stress. What did you learn today from Mary and Martha?

Week One Notes

What I Learned Today

Week Two

ORGANIZING YOUR CLOSET

Introduction
TAKING A CLOSET INVENTORY

A few years ago, I was helping a friend change out her closet between seasons. She had not worn many of the items; they either didn't fit or were out of style. When I arrived, I jumped right in and began to carry all the clothes from her closet to the bedroom so we could lay them out on the bed in order to go through each piece, one at a time. We went through every pair of shoes, as well as all the belts and purses. I asked her the same questions I ask myself:

- How long have I had this? Is it out of style?
- Has it been longer than two years since I have worn it?
- Is it a classic piece that will never go out of style? Will I be able to wear it for years to come?
- Does it still fit? If not, can I replace it for less than the cost of alterations?

After I had been there for several hours and we were almost finished, she began to notice some of the items in the give-away bag. As she questioned me as to whether she would possibly, but not likely wear them one day, I kiddingly said, "You get away from those bags." We both laughed. She only removed one sweater; I thought that was good considering we had eight bags of clothing.

We discovered belts that belonged to outfits long gone and purses that would make a thrift store owner very happy. Did I mention the hats? We had a lot of fun trying them on. At the end of the day, we felt good about what we had accomplished.

---

*R*egularly taking inventory of our clothing and cleaning out our closet will keep clutter to a minimum. I dare say most women, myself included, could go months without buying new clothing and still have plenty to wear from their overcrowded, bursting-at-the-seams closets. God asks us to be good stewards of what He has given to us. He also instructs us as women to dress modestly. 1 Timothy 2:9 says, "Women should adorn themselves in respectable apparel, with modesty and self-control…" ESV

If we as Christian women purpose to model godly character, we are to dress modestly. In the days ahead, we will discover how to be good stewards by shopping our own closets and receive tips that will help us in dressing to honor God.

FASHION, FRUGALITY, AND FAITH [3]

"Fashion is only as good as it looks on you." Author Unknown

With today's constantly changing trends and emphasis upon expressing sexuality through clothing, many godly women find it difficult to stay current with fashion without compromising their witness. The way we dress and present ourselves to others doesn't merely reveal our sense of style or personality; it shows what's in our hearts. How can we, as women, outwardly represent Christ and still have fun with fashion without breaking the bank?

WHAT DOES SCRIPTURE SAY?

- 1 Timothy 2:9-10, "Our focus should not be merely on the outward appearance but on who we are on the inside. Our aim in our dress shouldn't be to entice or impress others." ESV

- Proverbs 31:30, "Charm is deceptive, and beauty is fleeting; but a woman who fears the LORD is to be praised." CEB

- 1 Samuel 16:7b, "…the Lord looks at the heart." NKJV

- 1 Corinthians 6:20, "Honor God with our bodies." CEB

- 2 Corinthians 5:20, "We are therefore Christ's ambassadors, as though God were making his appeal through us." NIV

- Matthew 6:21, "Where your treasure is, there your heart will be also." ESV

SPIRIT CHECK—ASK YOURSELF THE FOLLOWING QUESTIONS:

1. Does the fact that Christ lives in me make a visible difference in my appearance?

2. Am I dressing to draw attention to myself? Am I honoring Christ in the way I dress?

3. Am I spending far too much money on clothing? Does keeping up with the latest fashion trends *hold* too much importance in my life?

4. Do I spend more time focusing on my outward appearance than my inward being—my heart?

Our society has gone casual, and there is nothing wrong with casual, if the occasion calls for casual. Styles come and go, but the one thing that never goes out of style is knowing the dress code for the environment into which you are entering, i.e., workplace, church, wedding, funeral, etc. On the following pages you will find: etiquette tips and clothing guidelines related to dressing for specific occasions, help with shopping your closet, and ideas for cleaning out your clothing closet regularly.

Let's begin with etiquette tips and guidelines related to dressing for specific occasions…

[3] *Pure Fashion Guidelines,"* last modified September 7, 2012, http://mayjesuschristbepraised.com/index.cfm?load=page&page=190

WHAT TO WEAR

by Linda Johnson

There are many things to take into consideration as we stare into our closets trying to decide *what to wear*. The time of year and the weather are two factors that dictate what we put on before we go out. Another is the occasion for which we are dressing. Different types of clothing will be appropriate for different types of occasions. For a Christian young lady, there is something else she must consider: Does God care what I am wearing?

HONORING TO GOD

> "Do you not know that your body is a temple of the Holy Spirit, who is in you, whom you have received from God? You are not your own; you are bought at a price. Therefore honor God with your body." 1 Corinthians 6:19–20 NIV

This scripture can apply to many areas of life, but Paul's main emphasis here was on sexual immorality. He exhorts us to glorify God in every aspect of our lives and in the usage of our bodies (temples of the Holy Spirit). Considering this exhortation, when it comes to our "temples" and what we wear we must ask these questions:

- Will the outfit I am going to wear draw attention to me or to Christ who lives in me?

OUR OWN FREEDOM

Our society tells women (and we believe it) that we can dress any way we want because our dress is not hurting anyone else. Paul saw our freedoms (our choices) as believers in a very different light. He penned God's thoughts in 1 Corinthians: "Everything is permissible—but not everything is beneficial. Everything is permissible—but not everything is constructive. Nobody should seek his own good, but the good of others." 1 Corinthians 10:23–24 NIV

We are reminded that our freedoms (our choices) should not cause harm to another. So we must take into consideration whether or not another person will be negatively affected by how we dress. Two results are possible if we make the choice to dress inappropriately:

- Men may stumble in the area of moral purity.

- Younger women will be encouraged by our example to dress in the same inappropriate way.

We should set aside our freedoms for the good of others. When we take these two things into consideration and determine to be obedient to God's Word, then we will not have a difficult time making decisions about our clothing. When we are shopping, or when we are deciding what to wear to the next social outing, wedding, or shower, we will choose wisely. Keeping God's honor, others, and these guidelines in mind, consider the following rules of etiquette for what to wear on specific occasions.

WEDDINGS

The time of day will dictate the type of dress for most weddings. Attire should be dresses, skirts, or suits for a daytime wedding. If the wedding is held outdoors, you may want something a little more casual and shoes that are appropriate for lawn and garden areas. Clothing for evening weddings should be dressier, and jewelry can be more elaborate. Some invitations may tell you the appropriate dress. Casual: this is usually found on invitations to outdoor weddings. Cocktail attire: dress is usually more sophisticated and elegant. Black Tie optional: Men can wear a tuxedo and women can wear long, formal gowns if they wish, although not required. Black Tie: Men should be in a tuxedo and women in long, formal gowns.

FUNERALS

Black is always appropriate for a funeral, but other subdued colors such as gray, khaki, and navy are also acceptable. Women should wear a dress, skirt, suit, or dress pants and blouse. Shoes should be comfortable; jewelry should be understated and simple. It is interesting to note that several clothing consultants suggested that inappropriate clothing for women would be items either too tight, too short, or those showing cleavage.

OFFICE PARTIES/SUNDAY SCHOOL GATHERINGS

Most of these occasions will be casual, so wear comfortable clothes and shoes. Even a secular website recommended conservative clothing with no tight blouses or cleavage showing. Remember that you represent God to those in attendance, and your dress should honor Him.

JOB INTERVIEW

It is suggested that you find out what the office dress code is and dress with a slightly higher standard when you go for a job interview. If you cannot find out this information, then a conservative suit would be your best choice. Make sure that the skirt is long enough for you to sit comfortably. Shoes, jewelry, makeup, and hair should be conservative and professional. Do not take your cell phone, iPod, gum, soda, or coffee to an interview.

CHURCH

Remember that men and boys at church are just as vulnerable to moral temptation as those at work or on the street. As godly women, we are responsible to dress appropriately as an example to younger women and as a blessing to the men and boys we worship alongside.

DEFINING ATTIRE

You receive an invitation to an important gathering that says White Tie for the attire. What does that mean? A friend invites you to a party and says that the attire is Informal. What is Informal? One time, my husband and I were invited to a party, and the dress requirement was semi-formal. Mark and a friend of his, who was also invited, decided to wear their formal wear (tux, starched white shirt, bow-tie, cummerbund, and cuff-links) on the top half and a pair of jeans on the bottom. To them that was semi-formal. Everyone got a good laugh out of their definition of semi-formal.

White Tie: Worn on the most formal of occasions. Women wear a full length gown. Men should be dressed in black tailcoat (with vest), starched white shirt, bow tie, black slacks with satin strip and black patent shoe.

Black Tie: Women should wear a short or long evening dress or dressy separates. Men should wear a black dinner jacket, matching pants, starched white shirt, bow tie, and black patent shoes.

Formal: Same as Black Tie attire. Men can wear a nice suit and women a dressy two piece.

Informal: Can be interpreted many ways. Semi-Formal is a more modern term for what used to be called Informal. The traditional interpretation of Informal attire was one step below Black Tie, meaning women wore fancy cocktail dresses and the men wore a dark suit and tie. But, times have changed. It is best to check with the hostess to know what is expected.

Business Attire: Women should wear a dress, suit, or pantsuit. Men should wear a business suit and tie.

Business Casual: In this day and time, businesses now have a very relaxed dress code. Always check with your host, but when in doubt, dress one level above what you think will be appropriate in order to look professional.

Dressy Casual: Guidelines for Business Casual may also be used for Dressy Casual. Women can wear a skirt, sweater, nice dress shirt, jacket, dress, or pantsuit. Men can wear a sport coat or blazer with a polo or button-down shirt.

Casual: Casual attire can be a minefield, everyone has a different opinion. Check with the host.

No Mention of Attire: Use your discretion but keep in mind when and where the event is held, before deciding what to wear.

EASY STEPS FOR CLEANING OUT
Your Clothing Closet

Let me ask you a question. What is most important to you when selecting clothing for your wardrobe? Trend? Fabric? Color? Style? Design? Cost? If you chose one of these, you chose incorrectly. What should be the most important thing when selecting clothing for your wardrobe is fit. Do your clothes fit?

STEP ONE: Uninterrupted time to go through your closet, trying on each piece that is in doubt.

STEP TWO: Full-length mirror to view fit from every angle.

STEP THREE: Space for placing clothes in piles. Sort by: Donate, Toss, Clean/Mend, or Keep. Begin by removing anything that is worn out, stained, out of date, doesn't feel good, or doesn't work for your lifestyle.

STEP FOUR: When trying on the clothing items in your closet ask:

- Does this item minimize or camouflage any aspects of my figure that are not my favorites?
- Does this item highlight the positives of my figure?

STEP FIVE: A kind but honest friend—sometimes it helps to recruit a friend who will be honest with us about the fit of our clothes. A friend who would not let you go out in public in something that would ultimately embarrass you. Put all the *keepers* back in your closet by color, style, length, etc.

Shop Your Closet

Many of you may be asking, how do I shop my own closet? In order to shop for clothes, don't you need to spend money? Not necessarily!

STEP ONE: Once you have taken the time to try on every piece in your closet, and have discarded everything that did not fit correctly, you are ready to shop your closet. Less is better for successfully creating new outfits.

STEP TWO: Identify the holes in your wardrobe. Are you missing some basics, like a pencil skirt or a great fitting pair of jeans? Do you need a couple of "wow" pieces to round off your wardrobe? Do you have an "orphaned" *keeper* without any other items to go with it? Discovering where your "holes" are in your wardrobe will prevent you from spending money on unnecessary clothing items.

STEP THREE: Mix and mingle the *keepers* into different outfits—be creative mixing colors and patterns. Add in the basics purchased to fill in the "holes" in your wardrobe. Doing this is called *shopping your closet* and being a good steward!

EASY WAYS TO
Change Clothing Looks

Slacks: Want a slimmer silhouette? Pants pockets tend to bunch or bow out, adding width where women least want width. Have the pockets stitched closed by a tailor, or if you are handy, do it yourself. This will give you a streamlined look.

Coats and Jackets: Give your old coat or jacket a new life—change the buttons. Any blazer, coat, or jacket can be revived just by a quick switch of the buttons. Be creative.

Lost Belt: Have you lost your belt for that skirt or pair of slacks? Purchase a coordinating colored ribbon and weave it through the belt loops and tie ends in a bow. Different colors and patterns of ribbon will add interest to the piece of clothing.

Long Lasting Shoes: Before you even wear a new pair of shoes, take them to a shoe cobbler and have rubber soles and heel tips attached. The extra layers will protect your shoes and ensure that they last longer. Just Google the closest shoe cobbler to find the one nearest to you.

Flair: To add a little flair to an older piece of clothing, throw on a colorful scarf or a fun statement necklace.

Classic Clip-ons: I know, you are thinking no one wears clip-ons anymore, right? But, if you have inherited some jewelry from your grandmother or an aunt, use the clip-on earrings to spruce up a pair of evening heels. Clamp the costume-style sparklers onto a plain pair of pumps to make the shoes more festive. Position them slightly off-center for a contemporary look.

Ankle Boots: Don't make the mistake of thinking that because they are called a boot, they can only be worn when the temperature is below 50. Ankle boots can be a year-round accessory, worn with a short tunic dress they are adorable.

Old Jeans: Still fit at the waist but the holes almost meet one another at the thigh? Consider making shorts from your old jeans. With a sharp pair of scissors, cut jeans just at mid-knee. Either roll and iron in place at desired length or if you want a finished edge, use bias tape (fabric used to cover raw edges). You can make your own using a cute floral fabric or purchase bias tape, follow directions on package for covering the raw edges of the jeans.

Shells: An effortless shell is the ultimate layering piece. Do not throw any away. They are timeless in style. Keep a couple in solid colors in your closet year round. A cute flowy shell can change the look of a jacket or blazer.

Clothing Swap: At the end of each season, invite a group of friends over for a clothing swap. This is a great way to gain a new wardrobe without spending money.

Must Haves

Slip: This may seem like an old-fashioned clothing item, but it is a necessary one when wearing sheer fabrics.

Correct Fitting Bra: I have discovered over the years that a good bra is worth saving the money to purchase, if you can do so. Also, as embarrassing as it may seem, allowing an expert to help with the fit of a bra makes all the difference in the way your bra looks from the outward appearance.

Tanks: Flowy, loose, low-cut tops often require a tank underneath. Test each top by bending forward in front of a mirror. If you can see breast, everyone else will also. To be discreet and modest, wear a fitted tank underneath.

Correct Fitting Undergarments: If the outline of your undergarments can be seen from the outside, your clothing may be too tight, or you are wearing the wrong type of undergarment for your outfit. Check with a friend or family member before you leave the house or consult a full length mirror.

A Full-Length Mirror: Pull up a chair in front of a full-length mirror and sit down to see if what you are wearing is appropriately covering your undergarments when seated. Doing a 360 while standing in front of the full-length mirror will ensure that you have not missed anything inappropriate. I have seen women who obviously did not check the back view of an outfit. Always look to see how an outfit appears from the back since people will be behind you in line, etc.

SUPPLIES, FIXES, and Repairs

Zippers: If you are not wearing a pair of slacks, jeans, or a jacket because the zipper is sticking, rub the trouble-spot with a dry waxy lubricant, like lip balm, a candle, or soap. Do not get it on the fabric since it may cause a stain.

Stretched Out Cuffs: Are you not wearing a sweater because the cuffs are stretched out? For a temporary fix, dampen the cuff with hot water then dry with a hair dryer. The hot water and the dryer's heat working together will cause shrinkage. Sometimes, running a hot iron across the cuff is enough to contract the fabric for a while.

Hems: A quick fix can be done with most tapes, or for a more secure fix, use stitch witchery (no-sew hemming alternative found in fabric stores or fabric departments of a store) or use a needle and thread.

Buttons: Always store extra buttons from clothing in case one comes loose or falls off. Sew in the direction of the threads of the remaining buttons on the garment.

Sewing Kit: If you don't have a regular sized sewing kit, purchase a small compact one at the dollar store, or pick up the free one in the hotel room the next time you travel. Having this handy can save frustration when your button is lose or falls off.

Stitch Witchery: This is a two-minute miracle worker sold at craft and fabric stores which makes fabric stick to itself to form a permanent bond. It does wonders for fallen hems and pocket flaps that won't stay closed.

Mini Scissors: Keep a pair of small scissors on hand to safely remove tags, washing labels, and loose threads.

THRIFT STORE SHOPPING

WHAT THRIFT STORES ARE IN YOUR CITY?

Thrift Shopping in Memphis:

GOODWILL: 3830 Austin Peay Highway, Memphis, Tennessee 38128

SALVATION ARMY: 3329 Austin Peay Highway, Memphis, Tennessee 38128

GOODWILL: 1740 Whitten Road, Memphis, Tennessee 38134

SALVATION ARMY: 2649 Kirby-Whitten Road, Memphis, Tennessee 38133

DAV (Disabled American Veterans): 3440 Summer Avenue, Memphis, Tennessee 38122

MIDSOUTH OUTLET: 3432 Summer Avenue, Memphis, Tennessee 38122

JUNIOR LEAGUE REPEAT BOUTIQUE: 3586 Summer Avenue, Memphis, Tennessee 38122

SUMMER OUTLET: 3466 Summer Avenue, Memphis, Tennessee 38122

CITY THRIFT: 5124 Summer Avenue, Memphis, Tennessee 38122

THRIFT STORE SHOPPING TIPS

1. Leave your purse in the trunk, and keep your money in your pocket.

2. Set a limit as to how much you're going to spend and don't persuade yourself to go past your limit no matter how good the "deal."

3. Look through everything in the store.

4. Look at items of clothing and furniture with an eye for potential. You can turn some pretty "useless" things into treasures if you really need them.

5. Get to know the cashiers, workers, and other shoppers. You'd be surprised at the community that you get to experience with fellow bargain shoppers.

6. Keep an ongoing list of items that you want or need and look for them at the thrift store until you find them.

7. Be patient; you'll appreciate the deal a whole lot more.

8. Find unique gifts you can give for birthdays, special occasions, etc.

RUTH
A Woman of Loyalty

Biblical Principle: When we are loyal, showing honor and respect to those older than us, we will receive God's blessings.

Read the book of Ruth.

1. What was Ruth's relationship to Naomi?

2. Naomi pronounces a blessing upon her daughters-in-law. What does this tell you about her walk with the Lord?

3. What were Ruth's feelings toward her mother-in-law? How do you know this?

4. Look up Exodus 20:12. Whether you have a mother-in-law at the present time or not, according to the verse in Exodus, describe how a daughter-in-law should treat her mother-in-law. God doesn't give any outs; you are to love, respect, and show honor to your parents and your in-laws, NO MATTER WHAT!

5. Ruth was a woman of obedience. She followed God's Word and showed respect, honor, and unconditional love toward Naomi. She is proof of the principle: *obedience equals blessings!* Because of her obedience, she reaped many blessings in her life. Name a few:

6. In what areas of your life, do you need to bow the knee to God's Word and obediently follow?

Week Two Notes

What I Learned Today

Week Three

TIPS ON LAUNDRY, IRONING, AND SEWING

Introduction

TO SEW OR NOT TO SEW

As I mentioned before, each of us four kids had responsibilities around the house. My brother did the yard with the help of my older sister. I enjoyed the indoor work. I can remember setting up the ironing board in the basement and ironing my dad's shirts for ten cents. My mom would starch dad's shirts with real liquid starch that she mixed herself. The shirts would soak in the starch, and then she rolled them up and placed them in the refrigerator overnight. The next morning she hung them to dry before ironing. I loved ironing, and to this day, I take pleasure in the finished product: a clean, fresh, crisp pair of khakis or a nicely pressed shirt. Ironing was my thing. I was good at it—but not sewing!

My mother-in-law, on the other hand, loved to sew. Over the years, she gave me two sewing machines. She hoped that I would love sewing as much as she did. But, I did not love sewing for several reasons. First, as a child all my clothing was either hand-me-downs or made by my grandmother. The second reason is the homemade dress I wore on the first day of fifth grade. My mother made it. The dress was olive green, covered with red fuzzy dots, and it had bell sleeves! Oh, it gets better! At that time, there was a fringe that was used mostly on kitchen curtains; it was a fringe with little fuzzy balls hanging from it. My mom decided to purchase the fringe in red and attach it to the edge of my bell sleeves. Did I mention that my mom wasn't a seamstress? It was quite a unique dress!

Another reason I didn't love sewing was a small part of the sewing machine called the "bobbin." You could lose your patience in a hurry with that little gadget—at least, I could!

The last reason was my attempt at sewing in my ninth-grade Home Economics class. Our teacher sent us to the store for a Simplicity pattern. Assuming the name meant simple, I got to work on my sleeveless sundress. I chose it because I didn't want to set in sleeves; I wasn't concerned with the fact that it was the middle of winter! Did you know that just because the pattern says Simplicity doesn't mean that it will be simple to make? Putting in darts was a real challenge for me, but eventually my sundress was complete. For our final grade, we had to model our creations while our teacher critiqued them in front of the entire class. I walked in the classroom door and turned to face the teacher. When I did, she pointed out that the darts were not even, and then she had me to stand in front of a mirror. Darts are to be right at the bust line, coming out from the side seam. Well, I got the dart on the right side pretty close, but the one on the left was about waist high—not good! I decided right then that sewing was not my gift! Even though machine sewing was not my gift, I made sure over the years that I learned how to hem, mend a seam, and attach a loose button to shirts and pants.

All I keep on hand now is my little sewing kit; that's all I need. No sewing machines for me!

Powdered Laundry Detergent

3 bars of soap—Fels Naptha®, Zote®, or Ivory® (these are marketed for laundry)

3 cups Borax®

3 cups washing soda/baking soda or Oxi-clean®

Place chopped soap in a food processor and process until fine. Pour into a large bowl. Mix with borax and washing soda; stir until combined. Use ¼ cup (same as four tablespoons) in HE front loader, use ½ cup in top loading machines.

FOR YOUR INFORMATION:

Use a mild soap, one with little to no additives. Castile soap is another good choice; it's made with 100 percent pure olive oil. Dr. Bonner's All-One Hemp Unscented Baby-Mild Pure Castile Soap is a good choice if there is a child with sensitive skin, such as eczema.

Washing soda is not the same as baking soda. Washing soda is an environmentally safe product that helps remove laundry stains. Borax is a natural deodorizer, stain remover, and laundry booster.

Liquid Laundry Detergent

1 Fels Naptha® bar of soap

4 cups water, boiling

1 cup washing soda

½ cup Borax®

Large pot

New 5-gallon bucket (purchase at any paint store, Lowe's® or Home Depot®)

Essential oils (optional)

Heat 4 cups of water until boiling. Grate Fels-Naptha® bar of soap with cheese grater and add to boiling water. Stir continuously over medium-low heat until soap dissolves and is melted. Fill your 5-gallon bucket half full with hot tap water, add melted soap, washing soda, and Borax®. Stir well until all powder is dissolved. Fill bucket the rest of the way to the top with hot water, stir, cover, and let sit overnight to thicken. The next day, stir well and fill an old laundry detergent container with detergent. Optional: add essential oils such as Doterra® Citrus Bliss. <u>Notes</u>: Detergent can separate, shake well before each use. Top load machines use ½ cup per load and front load machines use ¼ cup per load.

LAUNDRY TIPS

A few years ago, I was keeping the grandchildren while our youngest daughter and her husband were out of town. I began to notice that every morning the kids would put their pajamas in the dirty clothes basket. Now, knowing they had taken a bath before bed and then put on clean pajamas, I wondered why they threw their pajamas into the dirty clothes basket the next morning? I put a stop to that after the second day! Mimi was not washing clean pajamas just because it was easier for them to throw them in the basket than to fold and place them back in the drawer.

Many times we make more work for ourselves, or others make more work for us because of laziness. It is easier to throw what we have had on in the basket than to put it away. If you are clean when you put on the new clean item, chances are it is still clean after being worn once (except for summertime wear). Don't make more work for yourself—don't throw it in the dirty clothes basket just because of laziness. Train those under your roof to hang or put away clothing that can be worn again.

Laundry, as well as house work, can be daunting or just downright overwhelming! The bane of my youngest daughter's life is laundry. She loathes laundry. Yet, with a family of five and two boys playing baseball, she always has laundry!

Mounds of dirty clothes can seem like mountains you have to climb. If you don't keep up with the laundry, it can become a daunting task, one you loathe. Becoming knowledgeable about fabrics, ways to handle specific stains, and having a system in place will help as you tackle the task.

Perhaps with the following tips you will be able to climb the mountain of laundry, make the job less painful, and speed up the process.

UNDERSTANDING YOUR CARE LABELS

One of the first steps toward doing laundry quickly and efficiently is to know what each item is made of and the best way to care for it.

- Most garments have permanently attached labels. They can be a great help in determining exactly how you should remove stains and clean an item.

- Certain information is not required on care labels. Neither the manufacturer nor the retailer is required to inform a consumer that a certain fabric will shrink. The label assumes that the purchaser knows that an item labeled hand wash should be washed in lukewarm water by hand and that all non-white articles should not be treated with chlorine bleach.

- Another important piece of information contained on fabric care labels is the fiber content of the material. This is especially important with blends. These fabrics are combinations or blends of fibers, such as cotton and wool, cotton and polyester, or wool and acrylic. Blends should be cared for in the same way as the fiber with the highest percentage in the blend. Example: A blend of 60 percent cotton and 40 percent polyester should be cleaned as though it were 100 percent cotton. However, when you remove spots and stains you should follow procedures recommended for the most delicate fiber in the blend. Example: To remove a stain from a blend of cotton and silk, use the procedure recommended for silk. If after such treatment the stain is still apparent, follow the procedure for cotton, the most durable fiber in the blend.

CARE LABEL CHART

CARE LABELS

Machine wash	Wash, bleach, dry, and press by any customary method, including commercial laundering and dry-cleaning.
No chlorine bleach	Do not use chlorine bleach.
No bleach	Do not use any type of bleach.
Cold wash/cold rinse	Use cold water or cold washing machine setting.
Warm wash/warm rinse	Use warm water or warm water machine setting.
Hot wash	Use hot water or hot washing machine setting.
No spin	Remove wash load before final spin cycle.
Delicate cycle/gentle cycle	Use appropriate machine setting; otherwise hand wash.
Durable press cycle/ permanent press cycle	Use appropriate machine setting; otherwise, use warm wash, cold rinse, and short spin cycle.
Wash separately	Wash alone or with like colors.

NON-MACHINE WASHABLE

Hand wash	Launder only by hand in lukewarm (hand-comfortable) water. May be dry-cleaned.
Hand wash separately	Hand wash alone or with like colors.
No bleach	Do not use bleach.

DRYING

Tumble-dry	Dry in tumble dryer at specified setting: high, medium, low, or no heat.
Drip-dry	Hang wet and allow drying with hand shaping only.
Line-dry	Hang damp and allow drying.
No wring	Hang to dry or drip-dry.
No twist	Handle to prevent wrinkles.
Dry flat	Lay garment on flat surface.

IRONING

Cool iron	Set iron at lowest setting.
Warm iron	Set iron at medium setting.
Hot iron	Set iron at hot setting.
Do not iron	Do not iron or press with heat.
Steam iron	Iron or press with steam.
Iron damp	Dampen garment before ironing.
Dry-clean only	Garment should be dry-cleaned only.
No dry-cleaning	Garment cannot be dry cleaned.

Know Your Fabrics

NATURAL FABRICS

COTTON: Strong, long wearing, and absorbent. Will shrink and wrinkle unless given special treatment. Machine wash and tumble dry, using a water temperature ranging from cold to hot, depending on manufacturer care instructions. Chlorine bleach can be used on white or colorfast cotton unless a fabric finish has been applied. It is recommended that you use fabric softener to reduce wrinkling. The softener makes cotton less absorbent, so do not use on towels, washcloths, or diapers.

LINEN: Pure linen wrinkles easily; therefore, many manufacturers make linen blends or add wrinkle resistant finishes to overcome this problem. Machine wash and tumble dry linen; all-purpose detergent is the best cleaning agent. Chlorine bleach can be used on white linen, following the manufacturer's recommended amount so as not to damage the fabric. Linen can also be dry-cleaned.

SILK: Silk feels good to wear but requires special care. Most silk garments are marked dry-clean only. However, some silks can be washed by hand. It is suggested that you test a corner of the fabric for colorfastness before washing an entire garment; some dyed silk will bleed. Never twist or wring washable silks. Hang silks to dry. Press silk with a damp cloth and a warm iron, below 275°F, or use a steam iron. To remove stains from a washable silk, use only oxygen bleach or a mix of 1 part hydrogen peroxide to 8 parts water.

WOOL: Highly resilient, absorbent, and sheds wrinkles well, but wool will shrink and mat if it's exposed to heat and rubbing. It is recommended to treat stains on wool with solvent based spot removers. Wool should always be dry-cleaned unless it is specifically marked washable.

SYNTHETIC FABRICS

ACETATE: Closely related to rayon, has body, and drapes well. Taffeta, satin, crepe, and double knits often contain acetate. They should be hand washed using a light-duty detergent, if the care label specifies that the article is washable; otherwise, have it dry-cleaned. Use a press cloth when pressing the right side of the fabric.

ACRYLIC: Many acrylic weaves resemble wool's softness, weight, and fluffiness. Acrylics are usually wrinkle-resistant and are usually machine washable. They are often blended with wool and polyester fibers. Dry-clean acrylic garments or wash them by hand. If fabric is marked *colorfast*, it can be bleached with either chlorine bleach or oxygen bleach. Press at a moderate temperature setting.

NYLON: Is extremely strong, lightweight, smooth, wrinkle resistant, and nonabsorbent. Often combined with spandex, nylon knits are very stretchy but hold to their original shape. Always follow the manufacturer's cleaning instructions. Use chlorine bleach only when nylon article is colorfast, and use fabric softener to reduce static electricity. Tumble dry your nylon at low temperature setting and press at cool temperature setting.

POLYESTER: These garments are usually strong, resilient, wrinkle-resistant, colorfast, and crisp. They hold pleats and creases well, but are nonabsorbent. Polyester is used for clothing and filling; bed linens and towels are also made of polyester blends. It can be safely dry-cleaned or machine washed. Do not over dry polyester; this will cause gradual shrinking. Press all polyester fabrics on a moderate temperature setting or use steam iron.

RAYON: Is a strong, absorbent fabric, but it tends to lose its strength when wet. Used for draperies, upholstery, and clothing. Dry-clean rayon or hand-wash unless the label specifies to machine wash. Drip-dry and press rayon on the wrong side with an iron at the medium temperature setting while fabric is damp.

SPANDEX: Is a lightweight fiber that resembles rubber in durability. It has good stretch and recovery. Spandex blended with other fabrics provides the stretch in waistbands, foundation garments, swimwear, and dancewear. Hand or machine wash spandex-blend garments in warm water using all-purpose detergent. Line-dry or tumble-dry garments made with spandex at a low temperature setting. When removing from dryer, press clothing that contains spandex quickly at a low temperature setting.

LAUNDRY TECHNIQUES

Sorting your laundry is important and recommended for the safety of your garments and to shorten the time spent doing laundry.

COLORS: Sort laundry by color. Put all the whites or predominantly white articles together in one pile, light colors and pastels in another, and dark and bright colored clothes in another. Separate the dark pile into two piles: one for colorfast items (dyed in colors that will not fade or be washed out) and one for non-colorfast items (having a color that tends to fade when washed or worn).

DEGREE OF SOIL: Separate each pile into two smaller piles: lightly soiled and heavily soiled.

COMPATIBLE LOADS: Now you have up to twelve various-sized piles of laundry. Combine or divide the piles to come up with compatible, washer-sized loads.

The following five hints will help you with your final sorting:

1. Combine white and light-colored items that have similar degrees of soil into the same pile.
2. Combine the non-colorfast items with similarly colored colorfast items with the same degree of soil.
3. Create a separate pile for delicate items that must be hand washed.
4. Separate white synthetics, blends, and permanent-press fabrics from natural-fiber fabrics without special finishes.

Separate items made from fabrics that produce lint, such as chenille robes and terry cloth and bath towels, from fabrics that attract lint, such as corduroy, knits, synthetics, and permanent press.

PREPARING THE WASH

Follow these helpful hints to minimize damage to the articles and to clean thoroughly.

- Know fabric content so you can select proper water temperature and cleaning products.
- Save care information so you can follow the recommended cleaning procedures.
- Close all zippers, hook all hooks, button all buttons, and tie or buckle all belts and sashes.
- Mend seams, tears, holes, or loose hems to prevent future damage during wash cycle.
- Turn sweaters and corduroy garments inside out to prevent lint from attaching itself to the garment.
- Pre-treat spots, stains, and heavily soiled items with prewash spot-and-stain remover.

WATER TEMPERATURES

Sorting the clothing to be washed and understanding what temperature is best for each load will keep you from turning your undergarments pink or shrinking your favorite t-shirt!

THE TYPE OF LOAD	WASH TEMPERATURE	RINSE TEMPERATURE
White and light-colored cottons and linens	130–150°F	Warm or Cold
Diapers	Hot	
Heavily soiled permanent press		
Wash-and-wear fabrics		
All other greasy or heavily soiled clothes		
Dark colors	100–110°F	Cold
Light or moderately soiled permanent press	Warm	
Wash-and-wear fabrics		
Some woven or knit		
Synthetic fibers (see care label)		
Some washable woolens (see care label)		
Any other moderately soiled clothes		
Non-Colorfast Fabrics	80–100°F	Cold
Some washable woolens (see care label)		
Some woven or knit synthetic fabrics (see care label)		
Fragile items		
Bright colors		
Any lightly soiled clothes		

WASHING MACHINE: Clean the detergent depositing area of your washer. **For Dryers**: Clean out lint trap regularly. Two to four inches of lint is too much; you have waited too long! The lint trap is a fire hazard; it is very important for safety and the efficiency of the dryer to keep it cleaned out.

THREE TYPES OF STAINS

GREASY STAINS

- You can sometimes remove grease spots from washable fabrics by laundering; pre-treat by rubbing detergent directly into the spot or use dry-cleaning solution on the stain.

- If you are treating an old stain or one that has been dried and ironed, a yellow stain may remain after treatment with a solvent. Bleach can sometimes remove this yellow residue.

- To remove grease spots from non-washable fabrics, sponge the stain with dry-cleaning solution. Elimination of the stain may require several applications. Allow the spot to dry completely between sponging.

- Greasy stains may also be removed from non-washable fabrics by using an absorbent, such as cornmeal, cornstarch, French chalk, or Fuller's Earth® (mineral clay found in a local drug store). Dust the absorbent on the greasy spot. When it begins to look caked, it should be shaken or brushed off. Before using any of these products, carefully read the care label on the stained item and the label on the product container.

- If you do not have either one of these labels, it is recommended that you test the cleaning product on the fabric in an inconspicuous area. <u>Note</u>: As mentioned previously, Blue Dawn® dish washing soap worked into the greasy stain on clothing and then laundered works wonders!

NON-GREASY STAINS

- Non-greasy stains are easily acquired but not impossible to remove.

- If you are treating a non-greasy stain on a washable fabric, it is recommended that you sponge the stain with cold water as soon as possible.

- In the case of stains where the above process does not remove your stain try soaking the fabric in cool water. The stain may soak out within an hour, or you may need to leave the item in overnight.

- If some of the stain still remains after this treatment, try gently rubbing laundry detergent into it, and then rinse with cool water. The last resort is to use bleach, but always read the fabric care label before you use bleach.

COMBINATION STAINS

Some stains can be double trouble. For instance, coffee with cream or Thousand Island dressing and lipstick are a combination of both greasy and non-greasy substances. Getting rid of these stains is a two-part process. Get rid of the non-greasy stain and then attack the greasy residue. On most fabrics, you will need to sponge the stain with cool water, then work liquid detergent into the stain and rinse thoroughly.

- After the fabric has dried, apply dry-cleaning solution to the greasy part of the stain.

- Allow fabric to dry.

ADDITIONAL STAIN REMOVAL TIPS

- The quicker you treat a stain the better.

- The longer it sets, the more likely it is to become permanent.

- Know what you are cleaning, both the stain and the fabric.

- Remove as much of the stain as possible before cleaning the entire fabric to avoid setting the stain.

- Be gentle. Rubbing, folding, squeezing, twisting, and ringing can cause the stain to penetrate more deeply.

- Keep it cool. Avoid using hot water; heat makes some stains impossible to remove.

- Pre-test stain removers.

- Follow directions. Read manufacturers care labels and directions on products.

- Work from edges into the center to prevent spreading the stain or leaving a ring.

ADDITIONAL TIPS

- **Have a system**. If you have a large family, you may want to do laundry on M, W, and F. If you are single or newly married Saturday might be the best day for doing laundry. No matter the days you choose, set a system in place that works for you and stick with it. Systems relieve stress and frustration!

- **When using fabric softener sheets**, tear them in half to make them last longer and to help on your budget. It will not be less effective in keeping static from the load or making your clothes smell fresher.

- **No time to iron** when removing clothes from the dryer, hang them on hangers to keep the wrinkles to a minimum until ironing can be done.

- **When you can, set aside time to iron** those items coming out of the dryer. If you drop them into a basket until they can be ironed a week or two later, you will never know they have been cleaned. When you have freshly pressed clothing in the closet, getting ready will be much less stressful.

- **Sorting will save you time** and a lot of headaches. If you don't, you will end up with the fuzz from the throw rug all over your husband's black socks.

- **Ironing your husband's shirts** (especially the casual shirts) will save on the dry-cleaning bill. Using spray starch will improve their appearance.

- **For slips and nylon undergarments**, attach a small safety pin to the seam and you won't have a slip with static.

- **Purchase a mesh laundry bag** for washing small items such as bras, socks, etc.

Treating Special Stains

TO ELIMINATE ALCOHOL STAINS DUE TO PERFUME:

- Use a paste of baking soda and ammonia; test for colorfastness first
- Wear rubber gloves, and use this mixture in a well-ventilated area
- Dry the fabric in the sun
- Then wash it as usual

TO REMOVE BLOOD STAINS:

- Dampen the area with cold water
- Rub it with baking soda; test for colorfastness first
- Follow by dabbing with hydrogen peroxide until the stain is gone

POOL CHLORINE:

- Can be rinsed out of bathing suits in a sink full of water with 1 tablespoon baking soda added

CHEMICAL FINISHES in new clothes can bother sensitive skin. To remove the finish:

- Soak the new clothes in water and ½ cup to 2 cups vinegar
- Rinse them
- Add ½ cup baking soda to the wash load

DRY-CLEANABLE CLOTHES:

- Some dry-clean only items can be cleaned with a solution of 4 tablespoons baking soda in cold water. Test for colorfastness first

Baking Soda in Clothing Care

HOW TO USE BAKING SODA PASTE IN DOING LAUNDRY:

- Add ¼ cup baking soda with your detergent to freshen your laundry and help liquid detergents work harder

- For using baking soda in place of fabric softener, add ½ cup at the rinse cycle

- Add ½ cup baking soda (¼ cup for front load washers) with the usual amount of bleach to increase whitening power

PERSPIRATION STAINS:

- Scrub in paste of baking soda and water

- Let it sit for one hour

- Launder as usual

To treat stubborn perspiration stains around the collar:

- Mix a paste of 4 tablespoons of baking soda and ¼ cup water

- Rub it in

- Add a little white vinegar to the collar

- Wash the clothes

LAUNDRY OOPS!

Crayon in with a load of clothes:

- Rewash the load with the hottest possible water

- Add ½ to full cup baking soda

- Repeat if necessary

Stained your white clothes by washing them with colored ones, to undo the damage:

- Add baking soda, salt, and detergent to warm water

- Soak the clothing

- Rewash

Mending Tips

SUPPLIES TO KEEP ON HAND...

- **Scissors**—A small pair of sharp-pointed scissors will be useful for removing broken buttons, cutting thread, and trimming frayed edges. Keep your sewing scissors in a place where little or big hands cannot use them to cut paper or cardboard.

- **Seam Ripper**—A seam ripper can also be used to help remove broken buttons as well as removing stitching in order to make a repair.

- **Needles**—You can get by with two types of needles for basic mending. The #7 sharp needles have a round eye and are great to use with buttonhole thread. A #8 embroidery needle can be used for replacing invisible hems or other applications where all-purpose sewing thread is used. Both of these needles can be used for general sewing.

- **Thread**—All-purpose sewing thread in several basic colors should be a part of your repair kit. This thread will be 100 percent polyester. Machine embroidery thread is not suitable for basic sewing due to its lack of strength. A specialty thread known as buttonhole twist can be used to reattach buttons. It is very strong and only one strand of it needs to be used. This thread is available in a limited number of colors.

- **Fusible Interfacing**—Fusible interfacing is a product that is primarily used in the garment construction process, and it comes in several weights. A light-to-medium weight fusible interfacing can be used in mending tears in a garment by ironing it on the wrong side of the article to cover the tear.

- **Scraps of Fabric**—Small amounts of denim and soft woven fabrics from discarded clothing can be used to make repairs in blue jeans and other garments.

- **Iron-on-Patches**—Patches can be purchased from the fabric store to iron on to clothing to cover holes and tears. Patches are usually fairly stiff and are most often used on pants or jeans.

- **Stitch Witchery®**—A double-sided fusible material used to adhere two layers of fabric together. This product is sold in packages of narrow tape that can be used to repair hems. The glue is heat activated with an iron and care must be taken to avoid getting the adhesive on your iron or ironing-board cover.

JEZEBEL
A Woman with a Wicked Disposition

Biblical Principle: A woman with a wicked disposition seeks to destroy true worship, the family, morality, and the God-ordained role of male authority. God will not tolerate such a wicked spirit.

Read 1 Kings 16: 29–31 thru Chapter 21, 2 Kings 9:29–37 and Revelation 2:18–28.

1. Who was Jezebel? What type of woman was she? Describe her.

2. How did King Ahab acquire Naboth's vineyard? What part did Jezebel play in acquiring the vineyard?

3. Who was the prophet God raised up to confront King Ahab?

4. What did Elijah tell King Ahab would happen to him and his wife Jezebel as a result of their breaking God's law? (See 1 Kings 21:20-27)

5. A Jezebel spirit can be found in churches and families. In what ways does a Jezebel spirit manifest itself in the church? Within a family?

6. Prayerfully consider the following questions:

    - Do you seek within your marriage relationship to take control away from your husband, in the home and family?

    - Are you determined to have your own way?

    - Are you self-promoting?

    - Do you operate on a performance-based acceptance level?

    - Do you keep unhealed wounds from the past?

    - Do you dominate, control, and manipulate in order to accomplish what you want?

- Do you have a prideful spirit, an independent spirit, or a rebellious spirit?

7. Take a look in the mirror; do you look like Jezebel or are you a reflection of your heavenly Father?

*As in water face reflects face,
so the heart of man reflects the man.
Proverbs 27:19 ESV*

---

*Therefore be imitators of God, as beloved children.
And walk in love, as Christ loved us and gave himself up
for us, a fragrant offering and sacrifice to God.
Ephesians 5:1-2 ESV*

Week Three Notes

What I Learned Today

Week Four

ETIQUETTE

Introduction

DOS AND DON'TS

I was so excited. It was our first company function and in St. Thomas, of all places! Growing up, taking a family vacation to an exotic place was never an option. Now, I was going to St. Thomas, wow! I spent weeks purchasing just the right outfits and all on a young married couple's budget—so you can just imagine. Our last night in St. Thomas was to be a formal dinner. The dress I purchased was an empire-waist, scooped neck, taupe colored dress with the little white linen jacket. It was a knockout. Well, I thought so, anyway! I was so excited to get to wear it alongside this young, up-and-coming life insurance salesman, all decked out in his white tux. Yes, I said white!

That formal evening arrived, and we proudly went to the dinner all dressed up in our new attire, only to arrive to discover that Mark was the only man in a white tux. He was humiliated. My dress was great in my eyes but a little on the casual side compared to what the older women were wearing who were wealthier and more informed on dressing for formal dinners. We did notice one man in a formal black tux without any socks, but that didn't make Mark feel any better. Somehow, his sockless feet seemed a lot cooler and more socially acceptable than Mark's white tux!

Once we swallowed our pride, we entered the banquet hall and found our table. I looked down at the table setting to see four forks, three knives, several spoons of every size, and numerous glasses. My stomach was in a knot! What were all these utensils? I had never seen so many at one place setting. As I sat down, the waiter approached on my left and placed my dinner napkin in my lap. I gave Mark a look that said, *Help, what am I to do?* He smiled back at me as if to say, *It will be all right, follow me.* I was not sure I had a lot of confidence in the young man seated beside me in the only white tux in the banquet hall!

---

*T*he servers began to serve the first of many courses. I thought to myself, *I really don't have to eat. I could just sit here and be quiet, hoping no one would notice. I'm not really hungry anyway.* But I knew that would never work and might be more embarrassing than using the wrong utensil. I decided to watch Mark, and he decided to watch the others at our table. What they did, we did, hoping they knew what they were doing. They all seemed more seasoned than we were at this; they were very kind to us and tolerant of our minuscule knowledge of proper etiquette.

When I think back on our once-in-a-lifetime trip to St. Thomas, years ago when we were young, I get quite a chuckle. It is always easier to look back. I should have researched the proper attire for such a company function and studied up on proper table etiquette. But we live and learn, don't we? It is good to be informed.

You will always feel more comfortable in any setting if you are educated—thus the necessity of learning proper etiquette!

THE ETIQUETTE QUIZ

Before you take the etiquette quiz below, we need to talk about what etiquette is!

Etiquette is polite and proper behavior, using good manners, and being courteous. When I think of etiquette, I think of the word, R.E.S.P.E.C.T. A few synonyms for respect are words such as: considerate, thoughtful, showing esteem and regard for another.

Practicing proper etiquette is thinking of others first, being polite, using good manners, being courteous, being considerate, thoughtful, and showing regard or esteem for others.

Let's see where you rate when it comes to appropriate etiquette and showing respect toward others...

#1

WHEN SOMEONE SNEEZES YOU ...

A. Say, "God bless you"

B. Offer the person a tissue

C. Do nothing to acknowledge the sneeze

D. Ask if he or she is okay

#2

YOU RAN INTO A REALLY GOOD, OLD FRIEND YOU HAVE NOT SEEN IN FOREVER. YOU ...

A. Shake his or her hand

B. Give the person a hug or kiss

C. Wave and keep moving on

D. Pretend you do not know them

E. Offer a quick hello but do not make small talk

#3

WHILE DRIVING SOMEONE CUTS YOU OFF. YOU ...

A. Wave as a gesture that it is okay

B. Lay on your horn

C. Return the favor by speeding up and cutting the person off

D. Count to ten and try not to lose your cool

#4

WHEN YOU ARE IN A RESTAURANT OR A PUBLIC PLACE WITH OTHER PEOPLE AND YOUR CELL PHONE RINGS, YOU ...

A. Excuse yourself and step outside to not bother anyone with your conversation

B. Take the call and make an effort to keep it down/quiet

C. Wait until you get home to call the person back

D. Carry on as if you were in the comfort of your home

#5

YOU ARE BEHIND TWO PEOPLE IN THE GROCERY STORE CHECKOUT WHEN ANOTHER LINE OPENS UP. YOU ...

A. Let the people standing in front of you go

B. Race to the next line before anyone gets there

C. Wait a few seconds and give the people in front of you the opportunity to move before go yourself

D. Stay where you are

#6

WHEN SOMEONE GIVES YOU A PRESENT, YOU RESPOND BY ...

A. Sending a thank-you note

B. Saying, "Thank you" in person or texting (this does not take the place of a note)

C. Not saying anything

D. Refusing the gift

#7

YOUR DOG DOES HIS BUSINESS IN THE NEIGHBOR'S YARD. YOU ...

A. Only pick it up if someone is looking

B. Act like you do not notice

C. Pick it up with a plastic bag

D. Return to the scene of the crime after the fact

#8

WHICH OF THE FOLLOWING ARE YOU MOST LIKELY TO WEAR TO A WEDDING?

A. A black dress

B. A white dress

C. Any color but black or white
 (black is fine for evening wedding)

D. Who cares about color

#9

HOW MUCH SHOULD YOU USUALLY TIP YOUR SERVER?

A. I don't

B. 5%

C. 15% to 20%

D. About 30%

E. Depends on the service

#10

HOW OFTEN SHOULD YOU USE PLEASE AND THANK YOU WHEN ASKING FOR SOMETHING?

A. Always

B. Never

D. Most of the time

E. When I remember

#11

WHAT DO YOU DO WHEN YOU HEAR A JUICY TIDBIT OF GOSSIP ABOUT A FRIEND OR CO-WORKER?

A. Spread it around as quickly as possible

B. Only discuss it with close friends

C. Forget about it immediately

D. Ask the person concerned if it is true

E. Acknowledge the gossiper but don't contribute to the conversation

#12

IF SOMEONE SAYS SOMETHING YOU DO NOT HEAR, YOUR RESPONSE SHOULD BE ...

A. What?

B. Huh?

C. I'm sorry, could you please say that again?

D. "Excuse me!"

E. Nothing

#13

FOR WHOM DO YOU HOLD OPEN DOORS?

A. Anyone who follows close behind

B. Only women who follow close behind

C. Let the door close behind me without holding it open

D. Only for older people and those who cannot open doors themselves

E. People do not need any help opening doors; it is insulting to do so

#14

HOW MUCH TIME DO YOU ALLOW BEFORE YOU SEND A THANK-YOU NOTE FOR A GIFT OR KINDNESS YOU RECEIVED?

A. I never send thank-you notes

B. You should write and send thank-you notes immediately (there is grace for wedding gifts).

C. Whenever I get around to it.

D. Within a week of receiving the gift.

E. Within a month of receiving the gift (with wedding gifts, within six months of receiving the gift)

GENERAL RULES of Etiquette

HOSTESS GIFT: When you are either invited for dinner or for an extended stay in someone's home, it is proper to bring the hostess a gift. It should be a gift your hostess is not obligated to use that night, gifts such as candy, a candle, note cards, or a framed piece. A thank-you note can be left with the gift or written in the days to follow. This applies to occasions, such as showers and parties, given in your honor—take a gift and thank-you note for each hostess.

NAME GAME: In remembering names use the Rule of Three suggested by Nancy R. Mitchell in her book, *Etiquette Rules!* [4]

1. When you shake hands or in your first sentence of conversation repeat the name. "Hi, Jane."

2. Say the name again during conversation.

3. Say the name again as you say goodbye. If you didn't retain the name from the introduction, you may say as you are parting, "It was great talking with you about the organization. Thanks so much for the tip/information/sharing your thoughts. And, please tell me your name once more. I am sorry; it's been one of those days."

DON'T INTERRUPT: When people are talking: LISTEN. Don't interrupt. Effective listening takes work. To listen you must give your undivided attention to the person speaking. Being a good listener makes the person you are listening to feel cared about and special.

BODY LANGUAGE: Your body language can speak louder than words. It can convey a variety of emotions from anger, annoyance, comfort, insecurity, mistrust, stress, dominance, readiness, etc. Your posture, eye contact, gestures, facial expressions, placements of arms and feet, all deliver a message to others.

RESPONDING TO NEGATIVE COMMENTS: It is important to keep your emotions in check. Do not become defensive or allow yourself to be drug into a discussion with no possible resolution. Remember that negative comments or remarks are usually not directed at you, but at circumstances. If you are wrong, apologize and ask what the person would like to see happen or how the issue can be resolved, and clearly state what you plan to do. Do not take it personally!

RETAIL RUDENESS: Treat all sales staff with respect. Be courteous! Don't monopolize their time. When you have ten items and someone behind you has two, allow them go ahead of you. When a new register opens, allow the person in front of you to go first.

HANDICAP HELPS: Be courteous, not condescending. Offer a handshake. Offer help in general terms as you greet or escort them. "Please let me know if I can help. Look them in the eye, directing conversation to them. Use a normal tone of voice, they are handicapped—not deaf!

[4] Mitchell, Nancy R. "Etiquette Rules!." 2017. New York, New York: (Well Fleet Press.)

CELL PHONE ETIQUETTE

Cell phones play a leading role in our world and in our personal lives, from being a helpful tool to being a bad influence.

Turn off your cell phone, switch it to vibrate before sitting down to eat, or leave it in your purse. It is impolite to answer your phone during dinner, and even more impolite to text! If you must take a call, excuse yourself and step away from the table, or when eating out, go outside the restaurant.

Do not text in theaters, concerts, church, restaurants, meetings, public restrooms, or when you should be paying attention.

Do not text when engaged in face-to-face conversations, unless it is an emergency and you explain what and why you have to respond.

A text is not a proper way to communicate serious concerns, condolences, personal announcements, or gratitude.

Return a text message with a text message, not a call, because it is the initiators preferred method of communication. Always think R.E.S.P.E.C.T.

When texting for the first time, identify yourself. Be careful when group texting. Not everyone wants to receive every single response text. If you are engaging in an on-going conversation with one member of the group, switch to their private number.

Don't expect immediate responses and don't feel you have to respond in a nanosecond to every text. We are all busy and responses can wait! Sending follow-up texts to receive a quicker response is annoying. Don't do it!

DON'T say anything on social media that you would not say in person in a face-to-face conversation. The obscurity of the virtual world has brought out the dark side of many people.

Do not "overshare." Do not make every post about you. Do not share intimate details.

Tagging: Ask permission before tagging people in photos. If you are tagged and wished you were not, you can unlink a photo of yourself and then ask the poster to remove it.

Remember that technology is a means of communication—a tool—**not a part of your body**. Your iPhone, iPad, and laptop can be turned off, put away, silenced, and even left at home! Be respectful of those around you, those you love, and those you do life with!

PROPER ETIQUETTE
in a Social Setting

TABLE ETIQUETTE [5]

- Always pass food counter clockwise.

- When serving plates, serve to the left and remove the plates from the right.

- Napkins are placed in the center of the plate for formal dinners. Although, in a fine dining restaurant, the server will place the napkin in your lap.

- Napkins may be placed to the left of the forks with the fold facing away from the plate if a course is already on the table or for informal dinners. Unfold and place napkin in your lap. If you excuse yourself from the table, loosely fold your napkin and lay it to the left or right of your plate. Once you return, place it back in your lap. When the meal is finished, leave the napkin semi-folded at the left of the place setting.

- General rule for using the utensils is to start from the outside of your place setting and work your way toward the main plate.

- Foods you can eat by hand are bread, rolls, and muffins; slice or tear into small pieces before buttering.

- Foods that are meant to be eaten by hand are corn on the cob, lobster, sandwiches, certain fruits, olives, celery, cookies, and some cakes, spareribs, clams, and oysters on the half shell.

- When in a restaurant do not start eating until everyone is served. At a private dinner party, wait until the host or hostess picks up his/her fork to eat, then you may eat.

- Remember this rule: Eat to your left, drink to your right. Any plate to your left is yours and any drink to your right belongs to you.

- Knives go to the right of the plate, blade inward with spoons to the right of the knives. Forks go to the left of the plate.

- Once utensils are used, they must not touch the table; forks, knives, and spoons should be placed on the edge of your plate.

- When dining out, signal that you are done by resting your fork, tines up, and knife blade in, with the handles at five o'clock and tips pointing to ten o'clock on your plate.

- Glasses go above the knife on the right. Bread-and-butter plates go above the forks on the left.

- Filled salad plates go in the center of the plate, if served before the entrée; to the left if served with meal.

[5] The Taste of Home Cookbook (Reiman Media Group, Inc. 2009).

ADDITIONAL RULES OF ETIQUETTE

- Never excuse yourself from a dinner table and announce you are going to the bathroom; it is sufficient to say *Excuse me*, or *I'll be right back*.

- If right-handed, keep your left hand in your lap unless you are using it.

- Do not talk with your mouth full! This is rude and very distasteful for others to watch. Wait until you have swallowed to speak.

- Always say *please* when asking for something and *thank you* after receiving it.

- Whenever a woman leaves the table or returns, all the men seated should stand up.

- Always allow for the unexpected when determining your arrival time for a dinner party or event; it is rude to be early, so plan to arrive on time or no more than five to ten minutes late. Any later requires a call to the hostess informing her of your late arrival. Try to be punctual!

ETIQUETTE GOOFS [6]

1. Chewing or talking with food in your mouth.
2. Slurping, smacking, or making any unpleasant noise while eating.
3. Holding your utensil like a shovel.
4. Picking your teeth at the table.
5. Not using a napkin or failing to place it in your lap.
6. Drinking while chewing (unless you are choking).
7. Cutting up all the food on your plate at once.
8. Slouching over your plate or placing your elbows on the table while eating.
9. Using the *boarding house reach* instead of asking someone to please pass the food.
10. Leaving the table without saying *Excuse me*.
11. Applying makeup, except for a quick dab of lipstick done discreetly.

[6] The Taste of Home Cookbook (Reiman Media Group Inc. 2009).

CREATIVE CONVERSATION

Do you know how to word a question in order to have good conversations when out with friends or family?

These seven suggestions may help you in structuring questions when in a social setting...

1. Use questions that are easy to answer. For Example: How long have you lived in the area?

2. Use questions that are not offensive. For Example: Have you adjusted to the area?

3. Use questions that include everyone present—a question anyone could answer. For Example: As a child, what was your most embarrassing moment?

4. Use questions in which the people answering will not be judged by their response; people are reluctant if they feel their answer will be judged. For Example: Stay away from political hot topics, such as who your guests voted for in the last election.

5. Use questions that leave the person being questioned with a warm feeling—where they feel good about their answer. For Example: Questions dealing with family, trips/vacations, accomplishments, etc.

6. Use questions that create greater conversation among the group. For Example: Utilize the Fun Ice Breakers sheet.

7. Ask creative questions. For Example: Whom do you go to for advice?

    Remember...

    Creative and fun questions promote conversation and keep the energy going.

    Be sensitive to those who may be in a difficult place in life.

    Great questions are good for starting conversation, for helping to keep the conversation flowing, and are a way to get to know others better.

    Be well versed on a few topics; this will make it easier for you to enter into conversations.

FUN ICE BREAKERS

Choose any of the following to use in social gatherings to generate appropriate conversation.

1. Name one thing you miss about being a kid?
2. What did you enjoy most about school?
3. Who was your favorite music group in middle school? In high school?
4. When you were a kid, what did you want to be when you grew up?
5. What injuries did you have as a kid?
6. What was your worst dating experience?
7. As a kid, what was your most embarrassing moment?
8. Do you have any hidden talents?
9. Name one thing people do not know about you.
10. Tell about a funny family story from your childhood.
11. Was there ever a time you were frightened for your life?
12. What outdoor activity do you like to do?
13. Did you ever fight with your siblings? Who won?
14. What is your favorite place on earth?
15. What do you like about living in this area?
16. What do you consider the most important event of your life so far?
17. What do you consider your greatest achievement?
18. What is the one thing you would most like to be remembered for after your death?
19. Do you feel you have a calling or purpose in life?
20. Name three exotic countries you'd like to visit.
21. If your house was on fire and you could only grab three things, what would they be?
22. What do you value most in life?
23. What do you feel has been the greatest invention of all time?
24. What would be your dream job?
25. If you could live anywhere in the world, where would it be?

26. If you knew you were going to die in twenty-four hours, name three things you would do in the time you had left.

27. If you could go on a road trip with any person (dead or alive), who would you choose and where would you go?

28. What is your favorite verse in the Bible?

29. What is the most amazing thing you've discovered about God?

30. If you could be any one person from the Bible, who would it be? Why?

31. What has been your favorite book that you've read?

32. If you could take the place of a person in history, who would it be?

33. What is your favorite outdoor activity to do with your friends/spouse?

34. What is your greatest fear and what is one activity you would do if not for fear?

35. What was your favorite childhood Christmas memory?

36. What is the one toy you desired to receive as a child for Christmas, but never got?

37. What is your favorite restaurant? Your favorite ethnic food?

38. When you think of your childhood, what food comes to mind first?

39. Do you have a favorite memory of your grandparents?

40. If you were given $100,000, what would you do with it?

41. What is the greatest answer to prayer you have ever experienced?

42. When you get to heaven, what would you like to ask God?

43. If you could design and build your own home, what would it look like?

44. What is the single most important event you have attended?

ETIQUETTE FOR
Notes and Invitations [7]

THANK-YOU NOTES

- It is NEVER wrong to send a *thank-you* note!

- An e-mail or a phone call is acceptable for a close friend or relative, but a handwritten note is always the best form for showing appreciation.

- You should be prompt in your response to a gift.

- Always make the thank-you note personal, mentioning the gift by name and thanking the giver for his/her thoughtfulness.

WEDDING GIFT: A wedding gift must be acknowledged with a written note within three to six months of receiving it. Shower gifts also require a written thank-you note, even if you thanked the giver in person.

GET-WELL GIFT: Should be acknowledged as soon as the patient is well enough to respond.

CONDOLENCE GIFT: When receiving condolence gifts, (such as flowers or food) a personal handwritten thank-you note should be sent to the one who gave the gift. It is not necessary to send a note for a sympathy card if it is merely signed with the sender's name and brief words of sympathy.

CONGRATULATIONS GIFT: When you receive a congratulations gift (graduation from high school or college), you should send a personal handwritten thank-you note.

HOSTESS GIFT: A handwritten note must be sent after staying with someone as their houseguest. Taking or leaving a hostess gift during your stay is an especially nice way to say thank you.

REMEMBER: The giver has taken his/her time and effort, not to mention having spent their money in selecting a thoughtful gift for you. You should show proper gratitude and appreciation by sending a handwritten note.

In writing thank-you notes, follow this six-point formula:

Greet the giver—"Dear Aunt Sally,"

Express your gratitude—"Thank you for the gift card."

Discuss use—"I am going to use it to purchase bedding for my dorm room."

Mention the past, allude to future—"It was great to see you at my graduation and I hope to see you again soon."

---

[7] "How to Write a Thank You Note," last modified October 1, 2003, www.themorningnews.org/archives/how_to/ how_to_write_a_note.php

Grace—"Thank you again, for the generous gift." (It is not overkill to say thank you again)

Regards—"Love, Mandy"

RESPONDING TO INVITATIONS

RSVP (repondez, sil vous plait) means **RESPOND PLEASE!**

- Upon receiving an invitation, you must respond within a day or two; do not wait more than a week.

- You may decline an invitation, but never accept and then forget about it.

- If you accept, there are few excuses for not attending, barring illness, a death, or other major disaster.

- Keep your word; if you say you are going, Go!

Be sure to respond to wedding reception invitations since the host/hostess must plan on food for the proper number of guests. Be sensitive to those holding the event, if you commit to be there follow through on your commitment.

WRITING CONDOLENCES[8]

Often when tragedy and loss occur we do not know exactly what to say. But whether friend, family, co-worker, or acquaintance, you should always offer sympathy. Do not worry about saying the wrong thing. Just giving your condolences is the kindest thing you can do, as you acknowledge their loss and show that you care.

Think of writing a condolence note as a part of basic etiquette. Just as you would say please and thank you, you should express your sympathy in the form of a written note or letter to the bereaved. You may use a note card, a sympathy card, or a blank card for your condolences; remember, it is the thought that you put into words that counts.

Always give a lot of thought to your words expressed on paper or in a card. It does not have to be long. Your words should be simple and sincere. Below you will find a format to follow:

- Give a tribute to the deceased: pay your respects and provide a tribute to the dead.

- Offer the grieving your condolences: say to the bereaved how sorry you are for their loss. Be yourself and write as if you were speaking the condolences to them.

- Acknowledge their grief: you can acknowledge the grief has happened by offering whatever support you can and personally expressing your own deepest sympathy.

- If you knew the person who has passed away, write about a memory you have of them, or an act of kindness that they did for you.

- If you have some photos, you could include those in the note.

---

[8] Deborah R. Chappa, *Words for When There Are no Words: Writing a Memorable Condolence Note* (Haverford, Infinity Publishing, 1999).

THE RIGHT WORDS FOR CONDOLENCES:

- "We were sorry to hear about your great loss."
- "My thoughts and prayers are with you at this time of sorrow."
- "God bless you and your family during this painful and difficult time."
- "May God give you the strength you need to get through this difficult time."
- "May God bless you in this time of need."
- "During this time of sorrow, you are in our thoughts and prayers."
- "Our hearts go out to you."
- "May time heal your sorrow and memories sustain you."
- "In friendship and sympathy . . ."
- "We are remembering you and your family in our thoughts and prayers."
- "May the God of all comfort bring great comfort and peace to your hearts."
- Offer scripture verses that have ministered to you and your family in times of loss.

Remember that no words or gift will eliminate the pain of bereavement, but you can offer comfort, which is the precise reason we give them.

- Do not shy away from ministering to those who are hurting or determine you have nothing to offer.
- In times of pain and loss, we all need to be comforted.
- You can offer yourself, your words, your prayers, and your encouragement.

A Word from Dianne: I can personally testify that notes and cards sent following the death of a loved one, mean a great deal to those who have suffered the loss. For three to four months after Mark passed away, I received cards and notes. Not one word of encouragement and show of love was wasted. Each one along with the promise and assurance that they were praying for me brought comfort.

TAMAR
A Woman Suffering with Shame

Biblical Principle: Women do not have to live under the burden of shame, Christ came to set us free.

Read 2 Samuel 11:1–27 and 2 Samuel Chapter 13

1. Who was Tamar and how was she described?

2. Who was Amnon?

3. Amnon received bad advice. What was it and who was it from?

4. David requested that Tamar, his daughter, come and care for her brother, what was her response? What do you learn about Tamar from her response?

5. What was Amnon's objective in having Tamar come to his room? What was Tamar's response to her brother's advancements? Did he listen to Tamar's plea not to rape her?

6. How did Amnon feel after he raped his sister? How did Tamar feel?

Tamar carried shame with her the rest of her life. Today, one out of every six women in the USA is a victim of rape. Jesus Christ came to this earth as our Shame-Bearer. These women have absolutely no reason to be ashamed—hurt, yes, but never ashamed! God bears our shame. He is the One who punishes sin. It may seem that in this life, those who inflict such pain get away with it, but the Word says that one day they will give an account for the pain, hurt, and suffering they perpetrated.

If you are one of the many women who have experienced rape, know that your heavenly Father loves you, knows your pain, and desires to be your Shame-Bearer. He alone can heal your pain and take away your suffering.

Week Four Notes

What I Learned Today

Week Five

ETIQUETTE FOR CHILDREN

Introduction
THANK YOU!

When I was a little girl, it was *expected* of each of the four children in my family to set the table in the evenings before dinner. We ate together every night as a family. My mother taught us where to place the plate, glass, napkin, and utensils. Once we were shown, it was our responsibility to remember and to place each piece correctly. I grew up knowing how to set a table because it was *expected* of me.

We didn't eat at a restaurant as a family until I was a young teen. We didn't have the financial means to do so. But knowing my dad, I can tell you if we had been able to eat out, we would not have been running around the restaurant. We would not have been allowed to throw food or leave a mess for the bus boy to clean up. I know this because we were not allowed to act that way at home, so in public, we would have been *expected* to show the same respect for others that was shown at home.

Recently, I was visiting my niece, Jessica, her husband, Luke, and their two little boys, Micah and Levi. I told them that if they wanted to eat out, I would treat. I have never known a young couple who could turn down an offer like that! Luke chose the restaurant. Once seated, I anticipated that Jessica would pull out her iPhone for the boys, after all that is what young couples with kids (and without kids) do these days. But, she did not. In fact, she didn't even have toys or any objects to entertain them. The waiter brought a coloring sheet and crayons, the boys busied themselves with those for a few minutes. The service was slow that day, but at no point did Jessica or Luke resort to their iPhones to occupy the boys—instead they were expected to sit nicely until each one at the table had finished their meal. I was very proud of them for teaching their boys how to act in a restaurant—for expecting good behavior and getting it!

Other *expectations* my parents had:

- Address adults by Mr. and Mrs. or Miss. We were not allowed to call an adult by their first name unless given permission by the individual.

- To say please, thank you, yes ma'am and yes sir, no ma'am and no sir, when answering our parents or another adult, and to write thank-you notes for a kindness shown us.

- Respect of other people and their property. We were not allowed to walk through a neighbor's yard and certainly not allowed to ride our bikes through their yard.

These things my parents taught and demonstrated before me are called *Rules of Etiquette* or *Manners*. Manners are a person's way of behaving toward others, their way of speaking to and treating others. Perhaps your parents never taught or demonstrated these Rules of Etiquette, but you do not have to make that same mistake. Just Google the words *Children's Etiquette* and you can educate yourself and your children. You will reap the benefit and the blessings of having children who are well mannered—so will all those who come in contact with your children—as I did that day with Micah and Levi. You will only get the type of behavior from your children that is *expected* of them and that is modeled for them—who knows—one day they may thank you!

WHAT AM I TO DO?

What should a parent's response be to the child's behavior in each of the scenarios below? What rule of etiquette should be taught to the child?

SITUATION #1

You are in the play area at the mall with your children for two hours. Upon packing up to leave, you decide to have lunch in the food court on the level below. As you approach the escalator, your five-year-old son jumps in front of an elderly woman and almost sends her flying forward down the escalator. What in the world are you to do?

SITUATION #2

You and your family are in a restaurant with some friends and their children. It has been a long evening and the service is slow. The other children have been instructed to stay in their seats, but your children are getting fussy and want down. You finally give in so you can finish your conversation with your friends. Your children are running through the restaurant and almost knock over a waiter with a tray full of food. What in the world are you to do?

SITUATION #3

The phone rings and you have gone upstairs, so your eight-year-old son answers it. As you descend the stairs, you hear him say, "Yeah sure, hold on a minute." Then he slams the phone down on the counter and yells up to you to come get the phone. What in the world are you to do?

SITUATION #4

Your three-year-old daughter sees a candy bar she wants as you are checking out at the grocery store. You tell her you are not going to buy the candy today and she proceeds to throw herself down on the floor. The man behind you sees what is taking place and offers her a piece of candy from his pocket. She slaps it out of his hand. What in the world are you to do?

SITUATION #5

You and your two sons, ages four and six, are at the park playing on the swings when a little boy, age five, comes up and asks if he can please use the swing. Your four-year-old says no and refuses to get off. What in the world are you to do?

SITUATION #6

Your husband's parents have asked your children over for dinner. They have prepared all kinds of fun food and even planned ice cream sundaes for dessert. As you arrive to pick up the children, you hear your youngest complaining because they did not have the flavor of ice cream she likes. What in the world are you to do?

SITUATION #7

You are in the waiting room at the doctor's office and the children are playing. All is going well until you hear another child tell your son to shut up, and horror of all horrors, you hear your son tell the other child to shut up. What in the world are you to do?

SITUATION #8

Your family has been out to eat. As you are exiting the restaurant, your two oldest children decide to race out the door and run to the car. As they burst through the door, they almost knock over a young pregnant woman. What in the world are you to do?

SITUATION #9

You and your family are at a friend's home for dinner. After the prayer, your five-year-old reaches across the table and grabs a chicken breast off the meat platter and begins to dig in. What in the world are you to do?

SITUATION #10

You are at church and an elderly man comes up to your nine-year-old son and puts his hand out in order to shake hands and introduce himself. Your son refuses to shake his hand and hangs his head. What in the world are you to do?

SITUATION #11

It is bedtime and your four-year-old has just been handed a snack before bed, but refuses to say thank you for it. What in the world are you to do?

SITUATION #12

Your six-year-old daughter is having her birthday party. She opens a present given from a friend and begins to complain that it's not what she wanted. What in the world are you to do?

Answers: The proper responses to the above situations are found on page 94-95.

ANSWERS SHEET: WHAT AM I TO DO?

SOLUTION TO SITUATION #1

You apologize to the woman and ask her to wait at the bottom of the escalator so you can have your son apologize. When you get to the bottom of the escalator, you take him aside to explain. "First of all, as a young man and gentleman, *women always* go before men, and secondly, *older* people *always* go before younger people." You tell him he will have to go to the lady and apologize for jumping in front of her and almost causing her to fall. Walk him over to her and listen as he apologizes and then you apologize as well. Once he gets home, any further punishment is left up to you!

SOLUTION TO SITUATION #2

You and your husband should decide before taking your children out to eat what the rules are going to be. If your children are old enough to understand, explain the rules for eating out at a restaurant. You must train them to sit still and wait. Realize their limits—do not push them beyond their limits—especially if they are very young. Children should not be allowed to run around a restaurant. If the wait has been long and they are tired, maybe it is time to leave. If your children run into a waiter or waitress causing them to almost spill an entire tray of food, have the children apologize and then you need to apologize as well because you are the one who is really responsible.

SOLUTION TO SITUATION #3

Immediately apologize to the person on the phone. After finishing your conversation give your son a lesson in answering the phone correctly: "Yes ma'am, my mom is here. Just one minute please." You instruct him to lay the phone down gently and go to where you are to tell you that the phone call is for you.

SOLUTION TO SITUATION #4

You apologize to the gentleman and ask him to wait a moment after he pays for his purchase, so your daughter can say, "I am sorry." You take her aside and explain what she did wrong and that her behavior is unacceptable. Tell her, "We do not treat others that way and especially when they are offering us a gift. We are to thank them for the gift." Tell her she is to apologize for hitting him and thank him for the candy. When in the car, do what you deem best!

SOLUTION TO SITUATION #5

You go over and remove your three-year-old from the swing, explaining that when someone asks us politely to share with them, we are to share. After he has calmed down, have him apologize for saying no and for not being willing to share the swing.

SOLUTION TO SITUATION #6

You ask to be excused to another room along with your youngest and explain to her all the grandparents had done for her and her siblings that evening. Tell her that she is to be grateful and never complain about what others have freely and lovingly done for her; she is to always have an attitude of gratitude. Have her return to the room where the rest of the family is and apologize to her grandparents.

SOLUTION TO SITUATION #7

You approach both boys and explain that in your family you do not allow anyone to say shut up. Have your son apologize for his part. Once out of the waiting room, explain to him the level of disrespect that comes with telling someone else to shut up and that you will not allow him to do so, even when someone has said it to him.

SOLUTION TO SITUATION #8

You apologize to the young woman and ask if she will wait just a moment, while you get your children, in order for them to apologize. Call the children back, without screaming, if possible! Explain what they did wrong and ask them to apologize to the young woman. "I am sorry for almost knocking you down because we were racing to the car." After she has gone, explain to them that they could have really hurt her and the baby. Make it clear, you will not allow them to run out the doors ahead of you and race across the parking lot, and any time they run into someone they must apologize.

SOLUTION TO SITUATION #9

You apologize for him and ask if the two of you may be excused. Take him into another room and explain that he is to ask for the food he wants and wait for it to be passed to him. "May I have the chicken, please." Reintroduce him to silverware and its usage. Return to the table and have him apologize to the hostess.

SOLUTION TO SITUATION #10

Apologize and ask the man to wait a minute. Take your son aside and explain that what he just did was rude. Tell him the proper way in which he should respond in this situation. Return and have him reach out to shake hands with the man and introduce himself. Work on this at home so that if it were to happen again, he will know what to do.

SOLUTION TO SITUATION #11

You are to explain: No "thank you," No snack! Tell her, she is to always say *please* when asking for something and *thank you* when she receives it. If she does not say *please*, she will not receive it. If she does not say *thank you*, it will be taken away from her. If she refuses to say thank you, you must take it away!

SOLUTION TO SITUATION #12

Before your guests arrive, have an etiquette lesson on receiving gifts. First, always say thank you. Second, never complain about any gift. Third, be grateful!

CHILDREN'S ETIQUETTE [9]

You know you are raising a gentleman and a lady if they know how to ...

1. Say please, thank you, and excuse me on a consistent basis.
2. Do not point out other children's lack of manners.
3. Always knock on a closed door, particularly one that leads to a bathroom or bedroom.
4. Remove cap or hat when sitting down to eat at a table in a home or restaurant.

Introductions and Greetings

1. Refer to an adult as Mr. or Mrs. until asked to do otherwise.
2. Greet and converse with adult friends and acquaintances in a friendly and courteous manner.
3. Shows respect by standing when introduced.
4. Performs introductions, using first and last names among peers and Mr. and Mrs. when referring to adults.
5. When introducing family members to others, explains the relationship. *"This is my mother, Mrs. Chadwick, and my sister, Lilly."*

Shopping, Offices, and Waiting Rooms

1. Stays close to parents when shopping or in other public places.
2. Not greedy with samples in a grocery store.
3. Does not badger parent or other adult to buy things.
4. Does not rummage around, exploring desks or closets, in offices, or peeking under doors in dressing rooms.
5. Gives seat to an adult in a crowded waiting room.
6. Uses trash receptacles in public places.
7. When entering buildings, open door for adults, elderly, and handicapped persons.

Plays Well with Others

1. Does not shove or hit.
2. Does not throw objects at another child.
3. Shares toys with other children.
4. Does not spit on other children.

---

[9] This section extracted from Kay West, *How to Raise a Gentleman—A Civilized Guide to helping Your Son Through His Uncivilized Childhood,* Revised and Expanded (Nashville, Rutledge Hill Press- Division of Thomas Nelson Publishers, Inc., 2001, Update 2012).

5. Waits patiently in line for turn at an activity.

6. Does not push or crowd other children in line.

7. Does not hog the swings, but takes turns.

8. Does not knock down another child's sand castle or mud fort.

Party Manners

1. Considerate of other children who weren't invited or just didn't attend a party by not talking about the party.

2. Greets and bids farewell to the guest of honor, and thanks parents for the invitation.

3. Makes an effort to include everyone in the fun and thanks every guest for coming.

4. Never tries to steal the spotlight at another person's party.

5. Participates in all the party activities if possible. Realizes that by accepting the invitation he or she should be a cheerful guest.

6. Does not ask for more of anything—drinks, pizza, popcorn, candy, cake, pony rides, laser tag games, or arcade tokens—unless offered.

7. Never says, I already have this, when opening a present.

8. Sends invitations through the mail, rather than backpack.

Dining In and Out

1. Washes hands and removes hat before coming to table.

2. Keeps all four legs of chair on the floor.

3. Keeps elbows off the table, does not chew with mouth open, or talk with mouth full.

4. Does not play with one's hair at the table.

5. Asks for salt or pepper to be passed, rather than reaching across the table.

6. Does not take the last helping without offering it to someone else.

7. When being served, does not refuse a dish unless allergic to it. Instead, asks for a very small amount.

8. Does not eat before others begin, before host is seated, or before the blessing.

9. Asks to be excused from table when finished.

10. Does not talk about dessert while everyone is still eating the salad.

11. When dining in a restaurant does not get up from the table and wander about.

12. Does not waste or play with condiments on the table.

13. Treats the server cordially and with respect, saying thank you when meal is delivered and when plate is taken away.

Traveling Manners

1. Shows respect and courtesy toward the parent driving carpool and does not engage in back seat verbal or physical jousting.

2. Removes all belongings from the carpool car.

3. Does not leave trash in another's car.

4. Does not try repeatedly to open a bathroom door that is clearly occupied in an attempt to hurry the occupant.

5. Leaves lavatory in better condition than found it.

6. Keeps volume of music at level not disruptive to others.

7. If someone holds the door open for him, he is to say "thank you."

Temper, Temper

1. Does not express anger, disappointment, or frustration by using bad language or insulting someone.

2. Does not express anger, disappointment, or frustration by throwing, kicking, hitting, biting, or breaking something.

3. If loses temper and does any of the above, needs to apologize as soon as he/she has calmed down.

4. Does not shout to get someone's attention, or pout, sulk, or cry to get what they want.

5. Never uses words like fatso, stupid, idiot, retard, ugly, when addressing another person.

CHILDREN'S ETIQUETTE
for Social Media

At the rate we are going, communication skills will be non-existent among young people due to the constant usage of iPhones. Sociability is now seen as a text, twitter, and snap-chat instead of face to face communication. Families are drifting further and further apart due to the influence of "outsiders" in their children's lives via social media.

Phones have become a part of a child's body, person, and identity. Many find it hard, and even impossible, to function emotionally or socially apart from their phone. Parents are ignorant of the new technology leaving them in the dark as to how to control this out-of-control iPhone usage. But, the good news is that you as the parent, ignorant or not, pay the bill and **you can set the boundaries**.

The price of your child's heart, soul, mind, and emotional well-being is too high for you not to set boundaries on their social media. A boundary is something that indicates or fixes a limit or extent. Even if your child doesn't understand that you are setting boundaries for his good, the ultimate responsibility for protecting their physical and emotional well-being, and controlling their behavior is the parent's job.

WHAT CAN PARENTS DO?

- PARENTS need to set the example. If the perception your child has is that your phone is more important than he is—his phone will become more important than you!

- Limit time on the devices (screen time) the child has access to in your home. You bought it, you make monthly payments on it—you control when it will be used. Define what is a screen.

- Make a list of rules and expect that they will be followed or the technology is taken away. Example: No cell phone out at school unless required by a teacher, no cell phone at the dinner table, no cell phone will be allowed to be taken into their bedroom, no texting past 8 p.m., no texting unless their homework is completed, etc. When your rules are broken—take the devise away for long enough to make an impression!

- There are many tracking and filtering systems that can be placed on all your devices. This will help you keep strict tabs on all the text, emails, tweets, and snap-chats your child receive. Example: Integrity Online, Accountable2You, Covenant Eyes, etc.

- Do not naively think that what is on your child's device is none of your business. As a Christian parent, it is your responsibility to monitor these for the safety and protection of your child.

- No device should be allowed at social gatherings: Church, party for friend or family, dinner, or eating out, etc.

ETIQUETTE FOR
Children's Devices

WITH FAMILY AND FRIENDS

1. **Ask permission**: An elementary-age child should ask the adult for permission to use the phone. This reinforces the idea that phone usage is a privilege.

2. **Be courteous** to those you are with; turn off your phone if it will be interrupting a conversation or activity.

3. **Private/Personal information** can be forwarded, so don't text it, especially in a group text. Example: Saying that their dad is on a business trip, or telling about a fight between them and a sibling, etc.

4. **Texting doesn't replace talking**. Children/Tweens should understand that texting should not take the place of one-on-one interaction with their friends/family. If your child is going to bond with his or her friends, you need to encourage their spending time together.

5. **Don't text in front of others**. Explain to your children/tweens that they should never, ever text another person while they're spending time with a friend. It's extremely rude at any age and can hurt feelings. **Only exception** would be the need to text either parent as to a ride or other important information.

6. **Text messaging** and phone etiquette requires children/tweens to think about how their actions make other people feel. Talk to your children/tweens about thinking their text through before typing it and pushing "send."

7. **Be kind**. Children/Tweens need to understand that they are responsible for what they text to other people. Teach your children/tweens to refrain from gossiping about others, trashing others, and being unkind in general.

8. **It's all about context**. Explain to your children/tweens that sometimes text messages are misunderstood because of a lack of context. The person receiving the text message can't see the sender's facial expressions or hear their tone of voice. Jokes and sarcastic comments may cause hurt feelings if they're passed along in a text message.

9. **Text at the right time**. Your child should refrain from texting during class, at church, dinner, the movies, a friend's birthday party, a funeral, or in other public settings. The same applies if your family is going out for a meal or enjoying an activity together. Also, no texting early in the morning or late at night. If you, the parent, control the phone during those hours of the day, it should not be a problem.

10. **Think before you text**. Teach your child/tween to refrain from texting a friend if they're in a fight or are angry with one another. Ask your child/tween to wait until they have calmed down. Encourage them to work things out in person or over the phone.

11. **Making a call**. Teach children/tweens to introduce themselves to whoever answers the phone

before asking to speak to their friends. Example, "Hello, this is Will. May I speak to Drew?"

12. **Answering a call**: The child/tween should use a polite tone when answering the phone. Once the person identifies him or herself, the child should ask, "Who would you like to speak with?" If the person is not there, particularly if it's a parent, the child should say that the person is not able to come to the phone at that time. As many parents know, children should never tell callers that mom or dad are not home.

13. **Upon answering**, the child should never give his or her first name or the family's surname. A proper greeting would be, "Hello, may I ask who's calling?" This immediately puts your child at an advantage and immediately puts an adult off guard.

14. **Ending a call**: Teach your child/tween how to end a conversation politely, with good manners. He or she should say, "My dad is calling me to dinner, so I have to go. But it was very nice speaking with you, Libby."

IN PUBLIC

1. **Control your phone**, don't let it control you!

2. **Watch your words**, especially when others can overhear you.

3. **Speak softly**. No one wants to overhear a private conversation.

4. **Keep it short and sweet**. Children/Tweens should keep text messages short and to-the-point. If a "conversation" goes on for more than a few minutes, encourage your child to pick up the phone and continue the conversation by talking with their friend.

5. **Don't make calls** in a library, theater, church, grocery or store check-out line, or from your table in a restaurant.

6. **Don't text during class/school**.

7. **When in public** and the phone must remain on and could bother those around them, instruct them to use the silent ring mode. If it does ring in public, move away to talk.

8. **Keep content in mind**. Teach your child/tween that they should never deliver bad news in a text message. Example: "I heard your soccer coach quit!" or "I heard you and Sarah had a fight."

9. **Texting is a privilege, not a right**. Texting should be regarded as a privilege, and your child/tween should know that bad behavior will result in the loss of that privilege. Remind your tween that part of the responsibility of using a cell phone is following the family cell phone etiquette rules. That's a responsibility of growing up.

10. **No annoying ring tones** will be allowed.

11. **When with a group** and expecting a phone call, teach them to warn the people they are with that they are expecting a call and, therefore, they will need to step away to receive it.

12. **Nothing take persistence over** (is more important than) **people**—especially an iPhone!

PARENT POINTERS

TEMPER TANTRUMS AND OTHER BEHAVIOR...

- Do not respond to a temper tantrum by giving a child what he/she wants or promising to give a treat if he/she stops.

- Do not respond to a temper tantrum with a blast of your own. Remember, you as the parent are to set the example!

- If your child is having a temper tantrum in a public place, remove him/her from other people's presence.

- Do not react to your child's bad behavior with similar bad behavior. If you have a child who bites, do not bite back so your child can see how it feels, or hit a child to stop the child from hitting. You as the parent are to set the example!

- Do your best NOT to raise your voice in anger to a child. You need to set a good example!

- Do not fight with your spouse in front of your children. You need to set a good example!

- If you lose your temper in front of your child, apologize; if you lose your temper with your child, apologize. You as the parent are to set the example!

- Accept apologies quickly and graciously when they are made to you.

- Get your children to school on time, properly dressed, and prepared with what they need for the day. Remember, you as the parent are to set the example!

- Let your children know that within the school the faculty and administration are in charge.

- Communicate frequently with your child's teachers about your child's behavior in class, regarding play and work. Discipline may need to be administered at home.

- During church do not whisper with your spouse, friends, or children. As the parent, you set the example!

- Pay attention to the service, including the sermon, and do not use the time as an opportunity to pay bills or catch up on correspondence, or text! As the parent, you set the example!

- Address the clergy with their proper titles. As the parent, you set the example!

- Get your children in the habit of writing thank-you notes as young as possible.

- In sports, teach your children that games are meant to be fun, and if his conduct is making it less so, he cannot play.

- Teach children to include everyone who wants to play in the game, even if abilities are not as good as others.

- Yield to the authority of coaches and referees. If they need parents' advice, opinion, or help, they will ask. As the parent, you set the example!

- Do not do anything to embarrass your child ... yelling at umpires or calling the child by a private family nickname when he/she comes to bat.

- Resist urge to run onto the field to check a child's injury, or to usurp the coach's game plan or question his decisions. Remember, you as the parent set the example!

RESOURCES FOR CHILDREN'S ETIQUETTE

365 Manners Kids Should Know: Games, activities, other fun ways
to help children learn proper etiquette by Sheryl Eberly

BOOKS FOR CHILDREN'S ETIQUETTE

A Kids Guide to Manners: 50 Fun Etiquette Lessons by Katherine Flannery

A Little Book of Manners: Courtesy and Kindnesss for Young Ladies by Emilie Barnes

Don't Behave Like You Live in a Cave by Elizabeth Verdick

Dude That's Rude by Pamela Espeland and Elizabeth Verdick

Emily's Everyday Manners by Cindy P. Senning

Emily Post's Table Manners for Kids
by Cindy P. Senning

*How to Raise a Gentleman—A Civilized Guide to Helping Your Son
Through His Uncivilized Childhood* by Kay West

*How to Raise a Lady—A Civilized Guide to Helping Your Daughter
Through Her Uncivilized Childhood* by Kay West

My Manners Matter by Pat Thomas

Teeth Are Not for Biting by Elizabeth Verdick

The Giggly Guide of How to Behave at School by Phlippe Jalbert

The New Christian Charm Course: Today's Social Graces for Every Girl
by Emily Hunter, Jody Capehart, and Angela Carnathan

You've Got Manners: Table Tips from A to Z for Kids of All Ages by Louise Eldering

DVD FOR CHILDREN'S ETIQUETTE

What Every Kid Should Know About Manners and Etiquette by Joel Swenson

HANNAH
A Woman of Sacrifice

Biblical Principle: When we choose to give God everything, it will cost us something—it will require a sacrifice.

Read 1 Samuel 1:1–28, 2:1-11, and 2:18–21

1. Who was responsible for Hannah's barrenness?

2. What was the nature of the relationship between Hannah and Peninnah?

3. To whom did Hannah pour out her soul, and what was her request?

4. Did God give Hannah what she was asking of Him? What were the conditions surrounding His answer to her prayers?

5. Hannah fervently poured out her heart before the Lord. Is there something you are asking of the Lord and you presently find yourself in a state of fervent prayer? Do you believe God can and will answer your request?

6. What was Hannah's sacrifice?

7. She was obedient in keeping her word to give Samuel back to the Lord for His service. She, too, is proof of: obedience equals blessings. What are some of the blessings God gave to Hannah?

8. What lessons have you learned from Hannah that you can apply to your own life?

Week Five Notes
What I Learned Today

Optional Week Five

SHOWER AND PARTY ETIQUETTE

Introduction
YOU'RE INVITED!

*T*here is nothing more rewarding than giving a party or shower in a friend's honor. When your closest friend announces her engagement or another friend and her husband announce that they are expecting their first child, immediately all your female friends begin to plan ways to celebrate. Most people love a party and a reason to gather.

Recently, I was asked to be a hostess for a "Sprinkle." My first thought was, "What is a Sprinkle?" I had never heard of such a party. I have heard of baby showers, wedding showers, engagement parties, birthday parties, and even spiritual birthday parties, but I had never heard of a "Sprinkle"!

Things have changed and so have parties and showers. A "Sprinkle" I was told is a lower-key gathering that allows friends and family to "shower" or "sprinkle" a pregnant woman with love and a couple of gifts (like diapers) without all the bells and whistles of a big shower. Now, in the South we do things fancy and big. Nothing I have ever been a part of has been low-key or without all the bells and whistles! Our daughter lives in Texas. I am sure those of us in Tennessee don't do it up as big as Texans, because everything is big in Texas—but we come close. So, we will see if the "Sprinkle" is just that—a "sprinkle" of gifts and love!

A couple of years ago, I was told that a young woman I knew (who was expecting) and her husband, were going on a Babymoon. "A what,?" I asked. My friend explained that many young couples these days take a sort of second honeymoon before the baby arrives—I guess because life is over when you have a baby, and you will never travel again. I am just kidding. But, when we were expecting our first child, we were just wondering how we were going to pay for the delivery; the last thing on our minds or that we could afford was to take a Babymoon!

---

*W*e can find a variety of ways and reasons to celebrate. I have over the years, attended or been a hostess for a *New Home* party, a *Blessing* party, *Graduation* parties, *Tea* parties, *Garden* parties, *Christmas* parties, *New Year's Eve* parties, *Gotcha Day* (adoption) parties, and a *New Job/Promotion* party. People like to attend parties; they are fun. Hosting a party, as any good hostess worth her hummus knows, can be exhausting. But, you don't have to go through the event running on empty. In the following pages, I will explain the proper etiquette for giving a party and shower, as well as provide you with a list of necessities, table decoration ideas, and recipes.

I am hopeful that the information in the pages to come will assist you in not only hosting a shower or party—but help you enjoy it as well!

You're Invited to join me. Get ready, this is going to be a fun lesson!

WEDDING SHOWER ETIQUETTE

Who may Host a Shower? Anyone can host a shower. Years ago, it was thought unacceptable for a family member to host a shower for the engaged couple. But, times have changed, and it is appropriate under certain circumstances. Example: The bride is visiting her future in-laws and the groom's mother and sister want to invite the hometown friends and family to meet her. Let individual circumstances be your guide.

Must bridesmaids host a shower? Contrary to what you have heard, bridesmaids and the maid/matron of honor are not required to host a shower as a part of their "official" responsibilities. They certainly can if they want to.

When should a shower be held? The perfect timing is three months to two weeks prior to the wedding—after the couples plans are firmly in place.

How many showers can be given? Multiple showers are okay, but make sure you invite different guests to each one. Only close family and members of the wedding party can be invited to more than one shower.

Is a couples' shower acceptable? Showers for both the bride and groom, called Jack and Jill showers, are acceptable. Also, showers just for the groom are a recent phenomenon. Couples or groom showers can be themed. Examples: Room of the Day, Hour of the Day, the Great Outdoor Shower, His needs—Her needs, etc.

Are shower guests wedding guests? Yes, typically anyone invited to a shower would be invited to the wedding. There are only two exceptions, one would be if a group of co-workers wanted to give an office shower for the bride even though they are not being invited to the wedding and the other is a destination wedding. When a destination wedding is chosen, a shower may be given for the bride and groom by a group of individuals not attending the wedding due to distance or the size of the venue.

If invited to more than one shower, is a gift expected for each shower? If you are invited to more than one shower, you are only expected to bring a gift to the first one—that goes for members of the wedding party, too.

What should be printed on the invitation?

- Name of Bride-to-Be and Hostess
- Location
- Date and Time
- Directions
- Phone number of main hostess

- R.S.V.P. (include information about how to R.S.V.P.) or Regrets Only
- Theme of the Shower (if applicable)
- Dress Code (if desired)
- When addressing, use formal name. Example: Dr. and Mrs. William S. Brown

Who should be invited? The guest list should be made up of the couple's close friends, family, and attendants. The host should consult the bride to make sure that shower guests are wedding guests.

How many should be invited? It is up to the hostess to determine the number of guests. A shower is to be an intimate gathering. It is not to rival the wedding.

When should the invitations be mailed? Four to six weeks prior to the date of the shower.

Which response is better, R.S.V.P. or Regrets Only? The phrase R.S.V.P. means Respond Please and Regrets Only means that if you do not reply, it will be taken as an acceptance—you will attend. The guests should respond when either of these responses is requested on an invitation.

Can registry information be placed in the shower invitation? Yes, it is fine for the hostess to include registry information with, but not on, the invitation. A registry list is a suggestion; but remember the choice of gift is always up to the giver.

How much should be spent on a gift? As with any gift, how much you choose to spend should have more to do with your relationship with the recipient and what you feel comfortable spending than with an arbitrary dollar amount. If you are not a family member of the honoree, a basic rule of thumb is to spend no less than $30 and no more than $50 on a wedding gift.

Can an encore bride have a wedding shower? If a bride has been married before, she may be given a shower. Other than her close friends and family, the guests list should not include anyone who came to a shower for her first wedding.

WEDDING SHOWER RECIPES

Menu Selection: The menu chosen will depend on the time of day that the shower is given. Example: If the shower is from 11:00 a.m. to 2:00 p.m., a lunch menu would be appropriate. Below are a few good recipes for a lunch menu:

Hope's Coffee Slush

3 cups brewed coffee, cooled

3 pints half and half

2 tablespoons pure vanilla

2 cups granulated sugar

Mix thoroughly the ingredients above. Place in two large plastic zipper-lock bags. Press out the air, seal securely, and lay flat on shelf in freezer. A half hour before serving (may require 45 minutes in the wintertime) remove from freezer. As ingredients soften begin to break into pieces, creating slush. Serve in slushy consistency. Note: Replace one pint half and half with heavy cream for richer slush.

Refreshing Punch

2 lemons, sliced

3 large oranges, sliced

1 (6 ounce) frozen lemonade concentrate, thawed

2 (25.4 ounce) bottles sparkling apple cider

1 liter club soda

1 tablespoon granulated sugar

24-30 ice cubes

Thinly slice lemons and oranges. Place in large serving bowl. Pour in the thawed lemonade. Mix thoroughly. Gently stir in apple cider and club soda. Add sugar to taste and stir until dissolved. Add ice and serve.

Baby Carrots with Herb Dressing

1 (8 ounce) cream cheese, softened

1 cup sour cream

4 green onions, (white and green parts), chopped

2 tablespoons dill

¼ cup parsley, chopped

2 teaspoons sea salt

1 teaspoon black pepper, ground

40 petite rainbow carrots

Using a food processor, place cream cheese, sour cream, green onion, dill, parsley, salt and pepper in the work bowl. Process until smooth. Refrigerate until ready to serve. Using six 8 ounce clear plastic or glass serving cups, spoon ¼ cup dip into individual serving cup. Stand four to five carrots in the dip around the outer edge of the cup. Serve immediately.

Pesto and Turkey Pinwheels

½ cup mayonnaise

4 tablespoons pesto

1 tablespoon Dijon mustard

5 large flour tortillas

2 cups Arugula, chopped

10 pieces Provolone cheese, thinly sliced

½ pound deli smoked turkey breast, thinly sliced

In small mixing bowl, combine mayonnaise, pesto, and mustard. Evenly spread 2 tablespoons mayonnaise mixture onto each tortilla. Sprinkle each with arugula. Top each with 2 slices of provolone and 3 slices of turkey. Roll up tortillas tightly, and wrap in plastic wrap. Refrigerate for 2 to 4 hours. Remove and cut tortilla rolls into one inch thick slices making colorful pinwheels. Can be refrigerated in an air-tight container up to 2 days.

Bacon and Cheese Dip

5 slices of bacon, cooked and crumbled

1 (8 ounce) cream cheese, softened

1 cup mayonnaise

1 (8 ounce) Swiss cheese, shredded

2 green onions, finely chopped

1 tablespoon garlic powder

4 buttery crackers, finely crushed

Preheat oven to 350°F. Cook bacon over medium-high heat until evenly brown. Drain, crumble, and set aside. In a small mixing bowl, mix cream cheese with mayonnaise until creamy. Stir in swiss cheese, onions, and bacon. Place dip into a small oven-proof baking dish. Bake for 20-30 minutes until bubbly and lightly brown around the edges. Sprinkle top with crushed crackers. Serve warm with crackers.

Chocolate Hazelnut Dipped Strawberries

Fresh Strawberries

1 cup heavy whipping cream

1 (12 ounce) can evaporated milk

4 (3.5 ounce) bars dark chocolate, chopped (Ghiradelli®)

½ cup hazelnut chocolate spread

In a medium saucepan, heat cream and evaporated milk over low-medium heat, stirring continually until bubbles form around the edges of pan. Do not boil. Remove from heat; add chocolate and hazelnut chocolate spread. Whisk until smooth. Serve immediately with strawberries. Note: Can also be served with Biscotti.

Mini Almond Cupcakes

2 Duncan Hines® white cake mixes

6 egg whites, room temperature

1 cup oil

1¼ cups water

2 tablespoons almond extract

1 (4 ounce) sour cream

Preheat oven to 350°F. Line two 24-cup mini muffin tins with paper liners. Sift the cake mixes in the bowl of an electric mixer on low speed until lumps are removed. Add all the wet ingredients. Mix on medium speed until batter is smooth, scraping regularly to remove dry mix from sides and bottom of bowl. Pour batter evenly into prepared muffin pans. Bake for 15 to 20 minutes, until a cake tester comes out clean. Cool on rack.

ICING:

1 cup butter, softened

1 cup shortening

2 teaspoons pure vanilla

1 teaspoon almond extract

¼ teaspoon salt

8 cups confectioners' sugar

6 tablespoons milk (use more if needed)

In large mixing bowl, beat together butter and shortening until smooth. Add vanilla, almond extract, and salt. Gradually add confectioners' sugar and milk, beat until blended and smooth. Using piping bag, ice mini cupcakes and top with two sliced almonds.

Mini Lime Tarts

6 tablespoons sugar, additional 2 tablespoons

2 egg yolks, room temperature and slightly whipped

1 medium lime, grated

⅓ cup lime juice

3 egg whites, room temperature

1 cup heavy whipping cream

2 tablespoons confectioners' sugar

2 (8 each) packages of mini pastry shells, freezer section of grocery

In double boiler over medium heat, mix 6 tablespoons sugar, egg yolks, grated rind, and lime juice. Whisk over heat until custard-like texture is formed. Remove from stove. Cool. In bowl, beat egg whites and gradually add in 2 tablespoons of sugar until stiff. Fold egg whites into custard until smooth. Whip heavy cream with 2 tablespoons of confectioners' sugar. Fold into custard until light and creamy. Cook pastry tarts according to package directions, let cool. Fill with lime custard filling and top with fresh whipped cream.

GAMES AND CREATIVE IDEAS

WHO SAID IT?

This is a fun interactive bridal shower game. This game will test your guests as to how well they know the bride and/or groom It is a perfect choice for throwing a couple's shower. **How to Play**: Prior to the shower, have the couple answer a series of questions. At some point during the shower, plan a time to read their answers aloud. The guests will attempt to guess whose response they think has been read by holding up a hand when the hostess says "Bride" or "Groom." The participant with the greatest number of answers correct wins!

T.P. WEDDING ATTIRE:

Utilize your guests' creativity with this fun and interactive bridal shower game. All you will need is a package of toilet paper rolls—a fashion expert might come in handy as well! **How to Play**: Divide everyone into teams and give them two to four rolls of toilet paper in order to create a wedding gown. Each team will need a model on which to create their luxurious gown. Give them fifteen to twenty minutes. As you play the traditional wedding march, have each team's bride model their gown. The winner will be selected by the bride-to-be. If you are having a couples party, divide the men and the women. Give the women several rolls of toilet paper and the men duct tape along with broken down cardboard boxes. Each team will have 15-20 minutes to dress the bride and groom in appropriate wedding attire. It is a fun way for your guests to interact.

BRIDAL PICTIONARY:

The Bridal Pictionary game is a fun way to test your guests' artistic skills! Divide the guests into two or three different teams and let the games begin! **How to Play**: You will need a large wipe-off board or pad of paper and some markers for each team. Cut about ten slips of paper and write a wedding-related term on each. Place the slips of paper into a basket or jar. Each team will take turns pulling from the container, giving each one a try at guessing the wedding term/word their teammate is trying to draw. The team with the most correct guesses wins!

BLESSING CARD:

Have each guest write a special blessing or a favorite scripture verse that would be an encouragement to the Bride-to-be.

"WHAT I WISH" CARD:

Have each guest write what they wish their mother had told them about marriage prior to their wedding. Draw cards out of a basket and read aloud. Allow the guests to decide who wrote each card. Place in an album for the bride-to-be.

ENVELOPES FOR THANK YOU NOTES:

As the guests enter the home, have a basket of envelopes from Thank you notes (of the bride's choosing) and a pen. Each guest will address an envelope complete with their home address. This will save the bride time and ensure that she gets her thank you notes written.

WEDDING SHOWER TABLE DÉCOR

Theme: Decide if the wedding shower will have a theme and decorate accordingly.

Flowers are always appropriate. Placing two to three dozen colored roses or tulips in a large crystal vase is eye catching for the center of the serving table. Using a variety of square glass vases and "bunching" or "clustering" flowers interspersed with crystal candle sticks or votives makes a beautiful presentation.

The Hostesses each have a variety of talents. If one is especially gifted in decorating, ask if she would be willing to decorate the serving table. The others will oversee the remaining responsibilities.

Food is a part of the décor, so keep that in mind when selecting your menu and serving pieces. You want color, texture, and interest in the recipes prepared and in the way in which they are displayed.

Keep It in the Family: Pay tribute to the bride's relatives by putting their old wedding photos on display for a creative bridal shower idea. Guests will love taking a look at the styles of decades past. To make the serving table even more whimsical and picture-perfect, affix the images to teapot lids using 6-inch pieces of artistic wire. Intersperse vases with soft pink and off white flowers among the family wedding photos. Using a lace runner will give your table a more vintage look.

Centerpieces can be simple and cost-efficient. Here are a few ideas:

- **Straws and Flowers**: You will need two bunches of mini carnations (or flower of choice) in a color that fits your décor, a large square clear glass vase (size or sizes to fit the serving table), and colorful small plastic straws. Tip the square vase on its side and fill it up with new straws. Stand upright and add tap water halfway up. Insert individual stems of mini carnations (or flower of choice) into openings of randomly selected straws. Multiple vases on a table make a stunning and fun display.

- **Spools of Twine**: You will need different sizes of twine balls with holes in the middle, small waterproof glass containers that will fit down in the holes of the spools, mini Chrysanthemum flowers (or flowers of choice) and a rectangular wooden tray. Insert the small glass containers into each spool of twine. Fill with water and place a cluster of flowers in each one. Arrange the twine spools on the wooden tray. Votives can be placed among the spools for a more cozy feel.

- **Field of Daisies**: You will need 8-10 Gerbera daisies, wooden twigs from your yard, wheat grass, ceramic bowl of your choosing, and a sharp knife. Turn the ceramic bowl upside down and place a square of wheat grass on top. Trim the excess along the edge of the bowl with a sharp knife. Flip the bowl right side up and insert the wheat grass disc into the bowl. Insert twigs to create a standing nest or cage for the flowers. Poke daisies into the grass using the twigs as support to keep them upright. Add water. You can make multiples for a large serving table or intersperse with other décor on table.

- **Candles**: Add radiant elegance to your bridal shower serving table by using the soft glow of candles floating in crystal clear round glass bowls. Fill the bowls with water and along with the floating candles, add pearls, acrylic crystals, water-proof LED lights, colored sand, or fresh flowers. A combination of any of these would be beautiful. Place the clear glass bowls atop a decorative round mirror to create a warm and inviting look. Add warmth to your table by interspersing votive candles among the clear glass bowls.

BABY SHOWER ETIQUETTE

When should the shower be held? A baby shower should be held four to six weeks before the due date, unless the Mother-to-be wants to have it after the child is born. If you are counting by weeks, 28-32 weeks is an ideal time to host a baby shower.

How many showers can be given? Multiple showers are okay, but make sure you invite different guests to each party. Only close family members of the honoree can be invited to more than one shower.

Is a theme necessary? No. But a theme can be helpful in assisting with the type of decorations chosen.

Who should be invited? Since the hostess bears the expense of the party, it is up to her to determine the number of the guests she is comfortable accommodating. The hostess should give the honoree the number and ask whom she would like to invite.

How many should be invited? A shower is to be an intimate gathering where the honoree has the opportunity to speak with each guest. Limit the guest list to family and close friends. No one coming should be surprised to find out that there is a baby on the way.

What should be printed on the invitation?

- Name of Mother-to-Be and Hostess
- Location
- Date and Time
- Directions
- Phone number of main hostess
- R.S.V.P. (include information about how to R.S.V.P.) or Regrets Only
- Theme of the Shower (if applicable)
- Dress Code (if desired)
- When addressing, use formal name. Example: Dr. and Mrs. William S. Brown

Can registry information be placed in the shower invitation? Yes, it is fine for the hostess to include registry information with, but not on, the invitation. A registry list is a suggestion; but remember the choice of gift is always up to the giver.

When should the invitations be mailed? Four to six weeks prior to the date of the shower.

R.S.V.P. or Regrets Only? The phrase R.S.V.P means Respond Please and Regrets Only means that if you do not reply, it will be taken as an acceptance—you will attend. The guests should respond to the hostess when either of these responses is requested on an invitation, but often they do not.

How much should I spend on a gift? As with any gift, how much you choose to spend should have more to do with your relationship with the recipient and what you feel comfortable spending than with an arbitrary dollar amount. If you are not a family member of the honoree, a basic rule of thumb is to spend no less than $30 and no more than $50 on a baby shower gift.

BABY SHOWER RECIPES

Menu Selection: The menu chosen will depend on the time of day that the shower is given. Example: If the shower is from 9 a.m. to 11:00 a.m., a brunch menu would be appropriate. Below are a few good recipes for a brunch menu:

Hope's Coffee Slush

3 cups brewed coffee, cooled

3 pints half and half

2 tablespoons pure vanilla

2 cups granulated sugar

Mix thoroughly the ingredients above. Place in two large plastic zipper-lock bags. Press out the air, seal securely, and lay flat on shelf in freezer. A half hour before serving (may require 45 minutes in the wintertime) remove from freezer. As ingredients soften begin to break into pieces, creating slush. Serve in slushy consistency. <u>Note</u>: Replace one pint half and half with heavy cream for richer slush.

Sorority House Casserole

1 pound breakfast sausage

6-8 slices Italian bread

¾ stick butter, softened

¾ cup mild Cheddar, shredded

¾ cup sharp Cheddar cheese, shredded

7 eggs, beaten

2 cups half and half

1 teaspoon onion powder

1 ½ teaspoons salt

1 teaspoon pepper

1½ teaspoons prepared mustard

Preheat oven at 350°F. Cook sausage, drain and crumble. Spread both sides of each slice of bread with softened butter. Place in 9x13 baking dish. Sprinkle with sausage and cheddar cheese. In a large bowl, combine remaining ingredients and pour over bread, sausage, and cheese mixture. Top with ½ cup shredded Cheddar cheese. Cover and refrigerate overnight. Bake for 40-45 minutes until golden brown. Serves 12.

Fruit Kabobs

Using five fruits of choice, cut into bite-size cubes. If using apples or fruit that will turn brown, toss in a tablespoon of lemon juice. Place alternately onto a wooden skewer and serve with a dip recipe.

COCONUT DIP:

1½ cups vanilla yogurt, 4½ teaspoons unsweetened shredded coconut, and 4½ tablespoons orange marmalade. Thoroughly combine the ingredients in a small bowl. Serve with fruit kabobs.

CHOCOLATE DIP:

One (8 ounce) package cream cheese, softened, ½ cup confectioners' sugar, ⅓ cup baking cocoa, 1 teaspoon vanilla, 2 cups whipped heavy cream. In a large bowl, beat the softened cream cheese until light and fluffy. Beat in cocoa, sugar, and vanilla. Once combined, beat in whipped cream. Serve with fruit.

Lemon Blueberry Mini Muffins

BATTER:

- ½ cup butter, softened
- ½ cup shortening
- 3 cups sugar
- 4 large eggs, room temperature
- 4 teaspoons pure vanilla
- Juice and zest of two lemons
- 2 teaspoons pure lemon extract
- 2 cups sour cream
- 4½-5 cups all-purpose flour
- 2-¼ teaspoons baking powder
- 1 teaspoon baking soda
- ¾ teaspoon salt
- 1½ cups fresh blueberries

Preheat oven at 375°F. Line two 24-cup mini muffin tins with paper liners. In mixing bowl, cream butter and shortening until smooth and creamy. Add sugar, blend well. Add eggs one at a time. Add vanilla, lemon juice, zest, lemon extract, and sour cream. Blend well; fold in our, baking powder, baking soda, and salt. Mix well. With a large spoon gently fold in blueberries. Using a muffin scoop, scoop batter into paper-lined muffin tins. Batter should be firm and not topple. If it topples it may need a small amount of our added. Bake until lightly browned around the edges and muffins are set to the touch, 15-20 minutes.

LEMON GLAZE:

- 4 tablespoons butter, melted
- ½ to ¾ cup half and half/milk
- 2 cups confectioners' sugar
- zest of two lemons
- ¼ cup lemon juice
- 3 teaspoons pure lemon extract

Melt butter in glass mixing bowl. Add milk and confectioners' sugar, blend well. Fold in zest, lemon juice, and lemon extract. Brush glaze over muffins while warm. Serves: 60-70 mini muffins.

BABY SHOWER GAMES AND CREATIVE IDEAS

BABY BLOCKS:

Using plain wooden blocks, acrylic paint and brushes, have each guest design a block for the new baby. Each one will be personal and colorful.

DIAPER ADVICE:

Using a box of newborn disposable diapers and a permanent marker, allow each guest to write a word of advice or encouragement to the mother-to-be.

BECAUSE I SAID SO:

On a slip of paper or small index card, ask each guest to write down a parenting saying or advice that they associate with their parents. Place them in a basket. Mix them up, and allow each guest to select one. Have fun guessing whose card was chosen and whether or not the guest has or would say it to her own child.

BABY BINGO:

Go to the www.pampers.com website where you can download Baby Bingo game cards. How to play: Print out one bingo card per guest. Remember, each person's card must be unique! Before you start receiving your baby shower gifts, hand each guest their card. Each card has a unique combination of baby shower gifts. Each time, a gift found on a guest's card is opened, the guests must cross it out on their card. The first person to cross out a diagonal, horizontal, or vertical line wins a prize!

BLESSING CARD:

Have each guest write a special blessing or a favorite scripture verse that would be an encouragement to the mother-to-be.

WHAT "I WISH" CARDS:

Have each guest write what they wish their mother had told them about child birth or what they wish their mom had told them about parenting. Draw cards out of a basket and read aloud. Allow the guests to decide who wrote each card. Place in an album for the mother-to-be.

ENVELOPES FOR THANK YOU NOTES:

As the guests enter the home, have a basket of envelopes from Thank you notes (of the mother-to-be's choosing) and a pen. Each guest will address an envelope complete with her home address. This will ensure that the mommy-to-be will get her notes written before the baby is delivered.

BABY SHOWER TABLE DÉCOR

Theme: Decide if the baby shower will have a theme and decorate accordingly.

Flowers are always appropriate. Placing two to three dozen colored roses or tulips in a large crystal vase is eye catching for the center of the serving table. If a girl, a spectrum of pink interspersed with dashes of white will remind those gathered of the little one to come.

Silver Rattles, Stuffed Animals, and Books can be used along with the floral arrangement to add a personal touch.

Trucks and Trains can be used for a little boy's arrival. If the parents of the daddy-to-be have kept any toys from his childhood, these would be very special used as a part of the table décor.

Dolls and Strollers can be used for a little girl's arrival. If the parents of the mommy-to-be have kept any toys from her childhood, these would be very special used as a part of the table décor.

Food is a part of the décor, so keep that in mind when selecting your menu and serving pieces. You want color, texture, and interest in the recipes prepared and in the way in which they are displayed.

Shower Hostesses each have a variety of talents. If one is especially gifted in decorating, ask if she would be willing to decorate the serving table. The others will oversee the remaining responsibilities.

You are My Sunshine. Arrange bright yellow and white fresh flowers in glass jars. Colorful scrapbooking paper is good for making cute round tags with quotes or phrases that match the theme to attach to each jar. Using a gender-neutral color scheme of bright yellow, grey & white with chevron patterns will bring a touch of sunshine to the shower. A fabric runner matching the color scheme will add interest to the serving table.

Diaper Cake. These fun centerpieces are popular at baby showers because they double as practical gifts and centerpieces. The cakes are not difficult to make. It might require a little time, but you will save money in the end. The exact amount of supplies needed for a diaper cake depend upon how large you want the cake to be and how much money you want to spend on the project. Most diaper cakes use about 50 to 75 newborn or size 1 diapers. Below is a list of supplies:

- Diapers (disposable or cloth)
- Rubber bands
- Clear stretch jewelry cord
- Ribbon
- A cake topper (a stuffed animal, ribbon, board book, etc.)
- A sheet of cardboard, cake board, or a cake plate

Begin by preparing the diapers. Many diaper cakes are made with disposable diapers, but you can swap them for cloth diapers if that's what the mother-to-be prefers.

- One at a time, roll the diapers up tight starting from the front of the diaper and rolling it toward the back. Secure with a rubber band.

- Cut a piece of clear stretch jewelry cord to the fit the circumference of the base layer of the diaper cake.

- Place items like baby lotion, baby wipes or toys in the center of the cardboard or cake plate and start inserting the rolled up diapers one by one until you've created a circular shape.

- Wrap the piece of stretch jewelry cord around the diapers to keep the base layer together.

- Add a second layer of rolled up diapers and secure with a piece of stretch cord. Make sure the diapers are close together. If you can see any gaps between diapers or exposed rubber bands, secure a piece of ribbon around the layer to disguise it.

- Follow these steps for building the remaining tiers.

Once all the tiers are secure and complete, decorate the diaper cake with board books, teething rings or other small items. Tuck them inside the ribbon or fasten them to the tiers with tape. This an opportunity to really personalize the project for the baby's mom and dad, so don't be afraid to get creative. If the baby's gender and name are known, you could include that as well. The idea is to make the diaper cake eye-catching and practical at the same time. You may also wish to include rattles, board books, teething rings, baby wash, baby lotion, diaper rash cream, baby wipes, baby bibs, or other items inside your diaper cake. Note: For a step by step video on making a diaper cake see: http:/watchmojo.com>video>id>8625.

Shower Hostesses each have a variety of talents. If one is especially gifted in decorating, ask if she would be willing to decorate the serving table. The others will oversee the remaining responsibilities.

PARTY ETIQUETTE

Party Etiquette and Shower Etiquette are quite similar. Much of the dos and don'ts depend upon the type of party being given. To ensure a successful party, planning is imperative.

Do not invite more people than you can comfortably seat.

When to mail invitations or call to offer an invitation:

- Three to six weeks for an anniversary party.
- Same day to two weeks for a casual dinner/party.
- One month ahead for a Christmas party.
- Three to six weeks for a formal dinner party.
- A few days to three weeks for an informal dinner.
- Three weeks for a graduation or birthday party.
- A few days to three weeks for a housewarming party.

Make the invitation simple and make sure it includes all the pertinent information: type of party, date, time, address, dress, etc.

A time schedule for preparing for your party may seem like folly, but whether the party is for six or sixty, it is a necessity. What to do:

- Write down a complete menu far in advance. Make a grocery list from the menu recipes chosen.
- Make note of which foods can be made in advance and frozen or wrapped and stored in the refrigerator.
- Prepare all the recipes that can be prepared in advance and store according to instructions.
- Note the serving dishes you will need for the menu planned. Make certain you have a serving piece for each dish.
- Determine if your party will be a buffet or a sit down dinner. Plan accordingly.
- Set the table a day or two in advance.
- If special decorations are involved, plan and prepare ahead for these.
- Make tea a day or two ahead. Coffee can be placed in coffee pot hours ahead and turned on before the dessert is served.
- A day or two ahead, check your ice source and begin to store extra ice in order not to run out the night of the party.

Décor: This will depend on the theme and purpose of the party—decorate accordingly.

The more prepared you are, the more relaxing the evening or event will be for your guests. Planning and working ahead will ensure that you as the hostess will enjoy your time as much as the friends and family you invited. We are to open our homes, sharing all God has given us with others.

"Contribute to the needs of God's people; pursue the practice of hospitality." Romans 12:13 AMP

DINNER PARTY MENU

Cajun Grilled Beef Tenderloin

1 (3½ pound) beef tenderloin
¼ cup hot sauce
¼ cup low-sodium teriyaki sauce
3 tablespoons Worcestershire sauce
1 tablespoon Creole seasoning

Cooking Spray
Sandwich buns
Mustard-Horseradish Cream Sauce
Arugula

Place tenderloin in a large zipper-lock plastic bag. Combine hot sauce and following three ingredients. Pour over tenderloin. Seal bag; marinate in refrigerator 1-2 hours. Turn bag occasionally. Remove tenderloin and discard marinade. Coat grill rack with non-stick spray and heat one side of grill while leaving the other side turned off. Place tenderloin on the unheated side. Close grill lid and cook for 30- 40 minutes, turning once mid-way through cooking time. Let stand 10 minutes before slicing. Serve topped with Mustard-Horseradish sauce or on buttered buns with arugula and Mustard-Horseradish Sauce:

MUSTARD-HORSERADISH SAUCE:

¼ cup prepared horseradish
1 cup heavy whipping cream

¼ cup Dijon mustard
1 tablespoon fresh lemon juice

Using a spoon and a fine wire-mesh strainer, press all the juice from horseradish. Set aside and discard juice. In a glass bowl, beat whipping cream with an electric mixer at high speed until soft peaks form. Fold in horseradish, mustard, and lemon juice. Cover and chill for an hour.

Oven-Roasted Squash

2 medium-sized yellow squash, sliced
2 medium zucchini, sliced
1 red bell pepper, thinly sliced
4 garlic cloves, minced
2 tablespoons olive oil

1 teaspoon salt
½ teaspoon pepper
1 ½ tablespoons balsamic vinegar
3 tablespoons pine nuts, toasted
8 fresh basil leaves, cut in thin strips

Preheat oven to 400°F. In a bowl, combine first 4 ingredients; drizzle with oil and sprinkle with salt and pepper. Toss and place vegetables on an ungreased jelly-roll pan. Bake uncovered for 10 to 20 minutes. Remove and toss with vinegar, pine nuts, and basil. Serve immediately.

Roasted Rosemary Potatoes

2 pounds potatoes

½ cup olive oil

2 tablespoons fresh rosemary

½ teaspoon nutmeg

Salt and Pepper to taste

Preheat oven to 425°. <u>Note</u>: If potatoes are large, cut into quarters. In pan, parboil potatoes until just barely tender. Drain and place in roasting pan. Add olive oil, rosemary, nutmeg, salt and pepper. Roast potatoes, turning occasionally, until tender and browned. Place in serving dish and drizzle seasoned oil from pan over potatoes. **Suggested potatoes**: Red, Yukon Gold, Fingerlings or Dutch Yellow.

Blueberry Pound Cake

2 cups granulated sugar

1/2 cup butter, softened

8 ounce cream cheese, softened

3 large eggs

1 large egg white

3 cups all-purpose flour, divided

2 cups fresh blueberries, frozen (thawed)

1 teaspoon baking powder

½ teaspoon baking soda

½ teaspoon salt

1-8 ounce carton lemon yogurt

2 teaspoons vanilla

Cooking Spray

½ cup confectioners' sugar

4 teaspoons lemon juice

Preheat oven to 350°. Beat first 3 ingredients at medium speed of mixer until well blended. Add eggs and egg white, one at a time, beating well after each addition. Lightly spoon flour into dry measuring cups; level with knife. Combine 2 tablespoons flour with blueberries in a small bowl and toss well. Combine remaining flour, baking powder, baking soda, and salt. Add flour mixture alternately with yogurt, beginning and ending with flour mixture. Fold in blueberry mixture and vanilla; pour cake batter into a 10-inch Tube pan or Bundt pan coated with cooking spray or oil. Bake for one hour or until toothpick inserted in center comes out clean. Cool in pan for ten minutes; remove from pan. Combine confectioners' sugar and lemon juice in small bowl, drizzle over warm cake.

Week Five Notes

What I Learned Today

Week Six

TIPS ON CLEANING

Homemade Spray Cleaner

MIX TOGETHER IN A SPRAY BOTTLE:

1 cup white vinegar

1 cup water

Use the vinegar and water spray to clean countertops, range surface, and all backsplashes. For bathrooms, use to clean countertops, floors, and exterior of toilet. For hard-to-clean soap scum, take vinegar and water mixture, heat in microwave until barely hot. Spray shower walls and door, let stand 10 to 15 minutes and then scrub. Will soften soap scum.

HOMEMADE CLEANING PRODUCTS[10]

The four products for healthy cleaning are: Hydrogen peroxide, white vinegar, baking soda, and rubbing alcohol.

- **Hydrogen Peroxide** and cream of tartar made into a paste is good for cleaning porcelain and stains.

- **Undiluted white vinegar** can be used to scrub the inside of toilet.

- **Baking soda's** mild abrasive action makes it a good substitute for harsh commercial scouring powders. Sprinkle on a damp cloth and tackle the ring around the tub, clean vanities, or the kitchen sink.

- **Baking soda** will solve your stopped-up drain problems. Just pour ½ to ¾ cup into the drain, use just enough hot water to wash the solution down. Let stand for 2 hours or overnight, flush thoroughly with hot water; it deodorizes as well.

- **Rubbing alcohol** is better than Windex.

Equal parts of white vinegar and alcohol in a spray bottle works great on glass, mirrors, chrome fixtures, and ceramic tiles. *Peroxide* is a great bathroom cleaner. Using a spray bottle, make your cleaning solution. Mix 1 cup white vinegar, 1 tablespoon baking soda, and 1 cup water. Shake to mix. For a more pleasant scent, add 15 drops of either tea tree, lavender, eucalyptus, lemon, or peppermint essential oils to the water and vinegar.

A Recommended Book: *Everyday Cheapskate's Greatest Tips* by Mary Hunt contains recipes for cleaning solutions for every part of the house.

---

[10] "Pantry Recipes for Homemade Cleaning Products." http://organizedhome.com/clean-house/pantry-recipes-homemade-cleaning-products.

Introduction
A NECESSITY OF LIFE

*R*ecently while at the gym, I saw a commercial where the little girl says, "My mom said that there is no use for her to clean the house until I leave for college." This may sound like a grand idea. Why bother cleaning when those living in the house, apartment, or dorm room with you are just going to mess it up? If you think about not cleaning at all for the span of a child's growing up years or for the entire four years of college, that is pretty disgusting. Who wants to live in that filth?

We talked about de-cluttering in Week One. Truly, de-cluttering your home or apartment makes cleaning much quicker and easier. The less "stuff" you have to move out of the way in order to clean, the quicker the process. Start with picking up and putting away everything that is not in its "normal" place; then you can activate your cleaning plan.

Just as doing laundry is more efficient when you have a plan or system in place—so is cleaning. Systems may change with the seasons of life. Different seasons will require different cleaning systems and schedules.

When in school or working full time, the cleaning may need to be divided between a few evenings and the weekend. Once you marry and have children, you may have to divide the areas of your home and clean as you can according to the children's sleep schedules, school schedules, and your daily commitments. Once they are grown and out of the home, you may want to hire a maid! Why not?

I used to think the entire house had to be cleaned in one day. But, as I have gotten older and have gone through different seasons of life, I no longer worry about accomplishing that. I have a system which works for me. Weekly, I divide the downstairs of the house into three areas over three days. Because no one lives upstairs, I clean the upstairs once a month. This system works for me.

Where would we be without systems? How chaotic driving, banking, and shopping, just to mention a few, would be without systems. As grand as it sounds not to clean your home until the children are grown or a student completes their college education, it is not practical. No one wants to live in chaos and filth. Finding the system and schedule that will work best for you—whether wife, mom, single, or student, is the key to keeping your home, apartment, or dorm room clean without becoming frustrated and overwhelmed.

A CLEANING PLAN

With the right cleaning strategy, you can keep your time spent cleaning to a minimum and give yourself the maximum time for friends, family, and things that matter most. You may choose to clean for an hour every morning, two hours after work, or all of Saturday morning. Just have a strategy and schedule that fits into your life.

Concentrate on one room at a time; do not run all over the house pushing dirt around here and there. Stick with one room until it is sparkling clean. You will have the reward of having completely cleaned one space and then you can move on to the next room.

There are everyday chores such as making beds, cleaning the kitchen floor, doing dishes, etc. Then there are the big tasks such as cleaning out closets, kitchen drawers, cleaning ovens, etc. You should have a routine for the regular cleaning chores and a schedule for the bigger cleaning jobs. Below is a general plan for cleaning a home daily and seasonally.

EVERYDAY CLEANING

- Remove all dirt from your floors with a small vacuum, broom, dust mop, or Swiffer duster.
- Wash dishes and wipe off countertops and cooking appliances.
- Empty kitchen trash can, if necessary.
- Wipe down bathroom sinks and bathtubs.
- Make beds and straighten rooms.

CLEANING AS NEEDED

- Vacuum carpets and hard-surface floors thoroughly with vacuum cleaner or dust mop.
- Vacuum upholstery and draperies with upholstery attachment to vacuum.
- Dust and/or polish furniture.
- Clean the stove and wipe out the refrigerator.
- Wash kitchen and bathroom floors.
- Clean toilets, fixtures, and bathroom mirrors.
- Change bed linens, every week or two.
- Empty all waste baskets.

SEASONAL

- Surface clean rugs and carpets, using a carpet-cleaning solution or an absorbent powder.
- Remove all wax, apply new wax, and buff hard-surface floors.
- Wash throw rugs.
- Shampoo upholstery furniture.
- Wash or vacuum lamp shades, wash walls, and woodwork.
- Dust books, pictures, and lamps.
- Clean mirrors, TV screens, picture frames, and art objects.
- Clean ovens, microwave, refrigerator, freezer, and other appliances.
- Wash bathroom carpeting and shower curtain.
- Organize closets.
- Turn mattresses, wash pads and pillow covers, and air or wash pillows.
- Clean storm windows, screens, and windows.
- Wipe ceiling fan blades and motors with a damp cloth.

YEARLY

- Vacuum rug pads and the back of rugs.
- Shampoo carpets, clean rugs, and turn rugs to equalize wear.
- Wash curtains, blinds, shutters, shades, and clean draperies.
- Clean closets and cabinets.
- Wash or dry-clean bedspreads, blankets, and slip covers.
- Clean out garage, basement, and workshop.

EMERGENCIES

- Using warm water first, remove spots and stains while they are fresh.

CLEANING 101

Systems and supplies are the main ingredients in keeping your home clean. A well-stocked cleaning closet is a girl's best friend. You will be more likely to start your cleaning and finish the task if you have all that you need on hand. The following is a list of tools and supplies you need to efficiently clean your home.

GATHER YOUR TOOLS AND SUPPLIES

- **Baskets or Rubber Container**—Used for carrying supplies from one room to another and for collecting items that have been left in the wrong room.

- **Scrub Brushes**—Available in an assortment of sizes—the type needed will be determined by the job to be done.

- **Buckets**—A bucket for mopping and a two-sided bucket to hold your cleaning supplies and rags; keeps them all together, saving you time and energy.

- **Chamois**—These are expensive, but when properly used, last indefinitely. Nothing absorbs water better than soft leather, so it is perfect for drying cars and windows. After using your chamois, wash in a detergent solution, rinse thoroughly, squeeze out the water, stretch it to full size, and place it on a flat surface to dry.

- **Cleaning Cloths**—Can be made from old t-shirts, worn out wash cloths, sheets, diapers, or towels. Cotton, linen, white, or light-colored fabrics are best. Guardsman's® One-Wipe cloth is great.

- **Hydrogen Peroxide**—Sanitizes surfaces without damaging them.

- **Mops/Swiffer Dusters**—Mops should have detachable heads for easy cleaning.

- **Rubber Gloves**—Protect your hands. Always wear gloves when using cleaning solutions.

- **Scouring Pads**—Made of synthetics and steel wool. Keep a variety on hand.

- **Sponges**—Have plenty on hand. Wash occasionally in a load where bleach is being used or run through dishwasher cycle.

- **Stepladders**—Have one that is at least three feet tall.

- **Window Squeegees**—Speeds window washing and are great when used on shower doors and bathroom tile. Keep one in every shower.

- **New Two-Inch Paint Brush**—Great for dusting off lampshades. Also good for cleaning chairs, railings, and pictures.

GATHER YOUR CLEANING AGENTS

- **All-Purpose Cleaners**—Remove grease and grimy dirt.

- **Ammonia**—Available in clear or sudsy form. It is a grease cutter, wax stripper, window cleaner, and general soil remover. It is not a stain remover. Note: You can buy scented.

- **Baking Soda**—Most versatile cleaning product available. Used in dry form, it acts as a very mild scouring powder that will not scratch delicate surfaces. Use it to scour dirty surfaces by adding water to make a paste. Combined with other ingredients, it makes a very good cleaning solution that always deodorizes.

- **Bleach**—Helps remove stains and whitens laundry—also excellent for killing germs.

- **Lemon Juice**—Bottled or fresh; provides a mild acid reaction needed in cleaning solutions.

- **Liquid Dishwashing Detergents**—Used for cleaning tasks in addition to washing dishes.

- **Vinegar**—White vinegar can be used to clean fabrics and other household projects.

- **Waxes, Polishes, and Oils**—Used to shine and protect wood, leather, brass, chrome, silver, glass, and other surfaces.

TEN SPEEDY
Spring Cleaning Tips [11]

- **Remove clutter first**—Clear off items from tables, floors, and other surfaces before you start cleaning so you can zoom through each room.

- **Rely on a few ingredients**— Clean floors with 1 cup vinegar and 1 gallon water (Do not use this solution on wood flooring). Spray a mixture of half vinegar, half water to clean countertop and sinks.

- **Use one cleaning tool at a time**—Grab what you need to handle the same chore, like vacuuming, throughout your home, then switch tools.

- **Use micro-fiber cloths**—With dry micro-fiber cloths, dust furniture. Wet and wring out another for wiping down mirrors and glass surfaces.

- **Only clean what is dirty**—Spot clean visible dirt; skip cleaning walls, inside windows, and hardwood floors if they don't look dirty.

- **Call in help**—Consider handing some cleaning projects off to the pros; they do it faster, better, and have all the right equipment. Best jobs to hire out: carpet shampooing, sealing tile grout, and window washing.

- **Be efficient**—Instead of removing everything from shelves and cabinets, move items to the right to clean the left side. Then move items to the left to clean right side.

- **Give yourself a deadline**—Set a timer for ten, twenty, or thirty minutes, and tell yourself you'll finish a task in that amount of time.

- **Avoid scrubbing**—Spray cleaner in bathroom sinks, the microwave, and refrigerator and let stand five to ten minutes to soften hardened-on gunk.

- **Take advantage of overnight hours**—Before going to bed, set your oven to clean. Similarly, pour toilet cleaner in toilet bowls, then just brush and flush in the morning.

---

[11] Donna Smallin, "10 Ways to Speed Up Spring Cleaning," Better Homes and Gardens (May 2011): 94. 116

LET'S TAKE IT
a Room at a Time

CLEANING WALLS

Most walls are painted with latex, which is easy to wash after it has cured or set for a period of time. Clean walls with a commercial all-purpose cleaner, or use the following recipe for a homemade cleaner: Mix ½ cup of vinegar, 1 cup clear ammonia, ½ cup baking soda, and 1 gallon warm water. Apply solution to the wall with a sponge and rinse with clear water. If your wall has a texture, use old socks rather than a sponge. The socks will not tear like a sponge.

CLEANING WINDOWS

You can avoid washing your windows if you keep your blinds or curtains drawn, but life without light is gloomy. So, if you like light and want to look out at the world, you will need to clean your windows twice a year, usually in the spring and in the fall. Recipe for window cleaner: Mix ⅓ cup ammonia in 1 gallon of warm water. Apply with a sponge/squeegee or pour the solution into a spray container and spray it directly onto the windows. Wipe with a lint-free cloth, a chamois is best. Vinegar may be substituted for ammonia. Squeegees work well to remove excess water and then dry with chamois. <u>Note</u>: White coffee filters are great for cleaning windows and glass without leaving streaks or residue behind.

BATHROOM:

Bathrooms tend to become both dirty and messy. The obvious solution to bathroom clutter is first discard all unused items, then create storage for the things most bathrooms are not designed to store, such as hair dryers, makeup, electric shavers, and magazines. Using Rubbermaid containers, trays, and organizers can help with the bathroom clutter. The most efficient way to clean your bathroom is to clean it often.

- **Bathtub Rings**—A suggested method to keep bathtub rings from gathering on your tub is to add bubble bath to your bath water or a capful of detergent to the water. Towel dry.

- **Hair Removal**—Remove all hair from the tub and sink before cleaning in order to keep hair out of the cleaning cloth.

- **Cleaning Solution**—For tubs and sinks: This solution cleans porcelain as well as cultured-marble, ceramic tile, and fiberglass. Mix ½ cup vinegar, 1 cup clear ammonia, and ¼ cup baking soda in 1 gallon of hot water. Caution: Wear rubber gloves, and work in a well-ventilated area when using this powerful solution. Apply the solution to the fixtures with a sponge, scrubbing if necessary, and rinse with clear water. Dry with clean cloth.

- **Yellowed or Discolored Porcelain**—Clean with a paste made of cream of tartar moistened with hydrogen peroxide or a paste made of borax moistened with lemon juice. Scrub the paste into lightly stained areas with a brush and rinse well (old toothbrushes work well).

- **Ceramic Tile**—Stained or mildewed grout is very noticeable and makes your whole bathroom look dirty. A toothbrush or nail brush is the best tool for cleaning grout. To remove the mildew, dip the brush in chlorine bleach and gently scrub the affected grout. If spots persist, hide them by camouflaging them with white shoe polish. If you get the white polish on the tile, let it dry and wipe off with a damp rag.

- **Drains**—Moderately clogged drains can be treated by pouring ½ cup baking soda, followed by ½ cup vinegar down the drain. These ingredients when mixed create a foaming action. Let sit for three hours and rinse with clear water.

- **Shower Curtains**—Need to be cleaned on a regular basis to remove built-up scum, water deposits, and mildew. Most shower curtains are washable; fabric curtains and some plastic ones can be washed in the washer. Use regular detergent when you wash fabric curtains and follow the manufacturer's instructions for water temperature and wash/rinse cycles.

- **Plastic Shower Curtains**—When machine washing, use the gentle cycle and cool water. Wash plastic curtains in ½ cup detergent and ½ cup baking soda, along with two large bath towels. To prevent a machine-washed shower curtain from wrinkling, add a cup of vinegar to the rinse cycle. Washing the curtain in a bathtub will cause fewer wrinkles than machine washing. A good solution for cleaning plastic shower curtains is ½ cup vinegar, 1 cup clear ammonia, ¼ cup baking soda, and 1 gallon warm water. Apply the solution to the curtain with a sponge while it is lying flat. Wear rubber gloves when using this solution. Let the solution stand for several minutes to loosen scum, then scrub with a brush or sponge adding more cleaner if necessary. Rinse well with warm water to which a few drops of mineral oil have been added to make the curtain soft and flexible. Shake off excess water and hang to drip-dry, **or just buy a new one!**

- **For mildew on shower curtains**—Spray with disinfectant regularly. Shake excess water off curtain after every use.

- **Shower Area**—Spray periodically with a mildew inhibitor and disinfectant to cut down on mildew.

- **Leave the shower door slightly open** to allow air to circulate; this will discourage the growth of mildew.

- **Glass Shower Doors**—Sparkle when cleaned with a sponge dipped in white vinegar. A solution of white vinegar and water will remove hard water deposits.

- **Lemon Oil** is great for removing the water spots on the metal frame around shower doors.

- **If grout or caulking** breaks away, re-caulk immediately to prevent water damage.

- **Toilets**—A grin and bear it chore! In-tank cleaners are not a substitute for regular cleaning. Clean and disinfect your toilet bowl with ½ cup chlorine bleach. Pour it into the bowl and let it stand 10 minutes; scrub and flush. Wear rubber gloves and do not mix chlorine with other cleaners.

KITCHEN:

Kitchens get messy because they can be a "catch-all" place and because cooking can be messy! Below you will find some helps in keeping your kitchen clean on a regular basis.

- **Countertop Surfaces**—All kitchen countertops are made to be tough and durable. A variety of surfaces are available requiring different methods for cleaning. There are several popular countertops surfaces, among them are quartz, granite, marble, soapstone, solid surfaces, and butcher block. Each one should be treated differently:

    Quartz: Quartz has a nonporous surface that resists both scratching and staining. It is also impervious to heat and acid. No sealing is required. To clean quartz countertops you will not need anything more sophisticated than a gentle soap solution. Buff dry with a soft absorbent towel.

    Granite: Granite, a natural stone, is strong and durable. It will require sealing to avoid stains. It is almost impervious to heat. For cleaning, surface can be wiped with warm soapy water and rinsed. You can also use a 50/50 solution of isopropyl alcohol and water. Do not use vinegar, Windex, or bleach on granite.

    Marble: Marble is a natural stone and is waterproof and heatproof. It is not the best choice for kitchens due to its penchant for staining and scratching. To clean, you may use a marble cleaner or a squirt of non-abrasive dish soap with warm water in a spray bottle and spray counter generously. Scrub gently and wipe the soapy solution off with a clean wet cloth. Rub the counter dry and buff with a soft absorbent towel.

    Soapstone: Soapstone is a natural stone and is fairly impervious to heat. It should be wiped down with a damp cloth and treated with mineral oil regularly. After mineral oil treatment, you may use any household cleanser such as Ajax or Comet.

    Solid-Surfaces Materials: These materials are sold under brands that include Avonite, Corian, and Swanstone, and are all man-made material. Although they resist staining, they can easily be damaged by heat. Clean these surfaces with a damp microfiber cloth. A mild dish soap or ammonia based cleaners can also be used. Towel dry the surface to prevent water spots.

    Butcher Block: Butcher block countertops are very sanitary and waterproof when sealed. A thin layer of Mineral oil can be applied once a month for the first year, after that you can apply it once every six months or when surface appears dull. Clean by mopping up spills immediately with a damp cloth or paper towel. Adding a drop of liquid soap to your wet cloth will help loosen any sticky or greasy spills, making them easier to wipe up. Never use harsh cleaners like Windex, Formula 409, or any other chemicals.

- **Floors**—The first step to cleaning any floor is to get up all the dirt by vacuuming, sweeping, or using a Swiffer dust mop. A vacuum with a small brush attachment or crevice tool is effective in cleaning around baseboards, under refrigerators, etc. Knowing the material your floor is made of is important. Floors can be easily damaged by using the wrong cleaning method or product.

- **Dishwasher**—Baking soda cleans your dishwasher inside and out. Dip a damp cloth in soda and clean smudges and fingerprints from the exterior; (enamel surfaces) the same method will also remove stains from the liner. Use a synthetic scouring pad to clean stubborn stains and glass cleaner for chromium trim. For stainless surfaces use a combination of dish soap and baby or mineral oil. Going with the grain of your stainless, place a little bit of dish soap on an all-cotton cloth, moisten with a modest amount of warm water then wipe along the grain. When you finish cleaning an area, dry any water streaks with a clean towel or cloth. Time to polish. Dab a small amount of mineral or baby oil onto a dry towel. Follow the grain of your stainless steel. The results will make you happy.

- **Freezers and Refrigerators**—Regularly clean out and wash refrigerator and freezer to keep fresh and clean. For exterior, follow cleaning process described in manual.

- **Ceramic Cook-tops**—This is a glass cook-top with electric heating elements under the glass. Wait until the top cools to wipe up spills; never use a wet sponge or cloth on a hot panel. Abrasive cleaning products will scratch the surface. The best way to clean a ceramic cook-top is to sprinkle a nonabrasive cleanser or baking soda over the surface and rub with a synthetic scouring pad or sponge. Rinse well with clear water, and buff dry with a soft cloth.

- **Gas and Electric Stovetops and Ovens**—The exteriors of most gas and electric ranges are baked on porcelain enamel with chrome trim. Wipe the surface around the heating elements after each use. Use a synthetic scouring pad for stubborn soil. Harsh abrasives or steel wool will damage the stove's enamel or stainless finish. Gas burners should be washed occasionally. Clear the holes with a fine wire or pipe cleaner. Electric ovens are usually self-cleaning. All control knobs for stoves and ovens can be removed and washed in soapy water, dried, and placed back on appliance.

- **Stainless Surfaces**—Use a combination of dish soap and baby or mineral oil. Place a little bit of dish soap on an all-cotton cloth, moisten with a modest amount of warm water. Find the grain of your stainless and wipe along the grain. When you finish cleaning an area, dry any water streaks with a clean towel or cloth. Time to polish. Dab a small amount of mineral or baby oil onto a dry towel. Follow the grain of your stainless steel. The results will make you happy!

LIVING AREA:

- Remove all the clutter first. Everything in its place!

- Begin with higher objects such as ceiling fan, wall mounted televisions, light fixtures, fans, hanging lights, sconces, lamps, etc., using a Swiffer duster. Dust lampshades with a small dry, soft paint brush moving from top to bottom. Occasionally, clean these items with a cleaning solution according to instructions given on the object for removing dirt and grime.

- Dust all wood surfaces. I recommend using furniture polish once a month and a Swiffer duster the remainder of the month. This helps to prevent build-up. For furniture pieces that cannot be polished, use a slightly damp rag for removing dust.

- Shake out curtains, and when necessary, wash according to care label. Draperies will need to be vacuumed regularly or dry-cleaned.

- Clean all spots on carpeting, allow to dry completely, and vacuum.

BEDROOMS:

- Bedrooms tend to gather dust due to skin particles and because they are "lived in."

- Change sheets every week or every other, according to need. My grandchildren shower every night before bed and put on clean pajamas, because they go to bed clean, every other week is sufficient. If sick, you may want to change your pillowcases more often.

- Begin with higher objects, such as ceiling fan, wall mounted televisions, light fixtures, fans, hanging lights, sconces, lamps, etc. using a Swiffer duster. Dust lampshades with a small dry, soft paint brush, moving from top to bottom. Occasionally, clean these items with a cleaning solution according to instructions given on the object for removing dirt and grime.

- Dust all wood surfaces. I recommend using furniture polish once a month and a Swiffer duster the remainder of the month. This helps to prevent build-up.

- Shake out curtains and when necessary wash according to care label. Draperies will need to be vacuumed regularly or dry-cleaned.

- Clean all spots in carpeting, allow to dry completely and vacuum.

SPECIAL HOUSEHOLD
Cleaning Projects

MIRRORS

In order for the mirrors in your home to reflect well on you, they must be clean. Choose from one of these mirror cleaners to have beautiful, sparkling mirrors:

MIRROR CLEANER:

Mix 1/3 cup ammonia in one gallon of warm water. Apply the solution with a sponge/squeegee or pour into a pump bottle and spray sparingly onto mirror. Buff with a lint-free cloth, chamois, or paper towel. Vinegar may be substituted for ammonia.

MIRROR CLEANER:

Mix 2 cups isopropyl rubbing alcohol (70 percent), 2 tablespoons liquid dishwashing detergent, and 2 cups water. Stir until the solution is completely mixed and pour into a pump bottle. Spray the mixture sparingly on the mirror and buff with a lint-free cloth or paper toweling. Note: White paper coffee filters are great for cleaning mirrors without leaving streaks of residue behind.

TELEVISION SETS:

Your television collects dust and airborne particles. It is recommended that you use micro-fiber cloth on television screens. Note: With the new LED, HDTV, plasma LCD and QLED televisions, specialty cleaning instructions are given inside the instructional manual.

PICTURES:

Paintings and photographs framed behind glass require little care. When you clean the glass over a painting or picture, be careful not to allow any moisture to get behind the glass. When using furniture polish on picture frames, spray it on a cloth and carefully apply to the frame. Using a Swiffer duster works as well as polish.

BLINDS:

The best way to clean wood blinds is to begin with vacuuming the dust from each slat. With blinds turned in the down position, take a slightly damp cloth, and wipe each slat left to right. Depending on the degree of dirt, rinse the cloth every two to three slats and change water regularly. Turn blinds in the upward position and clean the other side. Natural wood blinds with decorative yarn tapes; should never be immersed. In most hardware stores, you can find a special duster designed for cleaning wood blinds.

CURTAINS:

Carefully read the care label on your curtains before determining method of cleaning; follow the manufacturer's instructions.

DRAPERIES:

Most draperies are lined and are usually made of fabrics that are much heavier than those used for curtains. It is usually best to dry-clean draperies. Vacuum all draperies before sending them out to be dry-cleaned. If you want to wash draperies, test a corner of the fabric in a bowl of warm water and detergent to see if it bleeds. When washing in a machine, use only the gentle cycle. Carefully read the care label on your draperies.

SHADES:

Light diffusing and opaque shades are normally made of fabrics that are washable; some have a protective vinyl coating that makes them easy to clean. Others are not washable and must be dry-cleaned. Vacuum shades regularly with the small brush attachment. Lower the shades completely before vacuuming to clean the full length. Do not forget the very tops of the shades and valances. To remove finger marks, use a damp sponge or a quick spray of all-purpose cleaner. Carefully read the care label on your shades.

SHUTTERS:

Vacuum all shutters regularly with the small brush attachment. Wipe them occasionally with a damp sponge to remove smudges and fingerprints. Use warm, soapy water with a damp cloth to wash painted shutters; wash each louver separately on both sides. Shutters that are finished with varnish, lacquer, or wax can be cleaned with commercial aerosol polishing/waxing products. Choose a product that is appropriate for the finish of your shutters.

FLOORING CARE

CARPET:

The easiest way to tackle vacuuming a carpeted room is to divide the room into sections. You can be sure to cover every inch of carpeting if you divide it into quarters and vacuum an entire quarter before moving on to the next. Vacuum once a week or more in areas of heavy traffic. Frequent vacuuming prolongs the life of your carpet. Every six months, vacuum around the edge of the carpeting along the baseboards. On occasion, do a deep cleaning of carpets to deal effectively with stains and spots.

CERAMIC TILE, GLAZED:

Highly glazed ceramic flooring is almost carefree floor covering. It requires little more than regular vacuuming and damp mopping. When damp mopping, use an all-purpose cleaner along with a synthetic scouring pad. Dry the floor with a soft cloth to avoid streaks. A bucket of water with 1 cup of white vinegar will make the floor glisten.

CERAMIC TILE, UNGLAZED:

Unlike shiny, easy-to-care for glazed tile, unglazed tile is porous and must be sealed to resist stains. Unglazed tile floors need to be sealed with a commercial sealer and a water-based wax. Do not clean your unglazed ceramic-tile floor with acids, strong soaps, or abrasives. Vacuuming followed by damp mopping should be sufficient.

MARBLE:

Non-polished marble is very porous and must be sealed with a commercial sealer. Polished marble is less porous but can still be stained. Marble floors look great after being damp mopped using clear water and an all-purpose cleaning solution in warm water, or a mixture of 1 cup fabric softener and ½ gallon water. If the floor appears to be dull after several washings, mop with 1 gallon water and 1 cup of white vinegar solution. It will glisten, and this beats re-waxing.

VINYL NO-WAX:

This flooring is a breeze to maintain. All you have to do is keep it clean. Vacuuming and damp mopping should be all that is needed. Use an all-purpose cleaning solution on vinyl floors and always read the product label for precautionary measures and instructions. It might be good to test any cleaner before applying it to the entire floor. If your no-wax floor loses its shine in high traffic areas, use a glossy renewing product available from the manufacturer of your floor.

WOOD:

Wood floors are elegant. The care of floors will depend upon the product that was used to seal the floor: varnish, shellac, polyurethane, or lacquer. Only the polyurethane requires no further treatment, including waxing. The integrity and beauty of wood floors not finished with polyurethane can be maintained by using solvent-based cleaners and polishes. Note: Water should never be used on wood floors, except those treated with polyurethane; these can be washed with a lightly damp mop. For varnished, shellacked, or lacquered floors, the fastest way to clean is with a one-step cleaner/polish.

Vacuum the floor, then pour the solvent-based liquid on a small area and rub lightly with a clean, dry wax applicator. Work a small section at a time; stroke the floor in the direction of the grain. Blot up any excess liquid with a clean cloth. Apply a liquid or paste solvent-based wax to wood floors twice a year. Make sure the room is well ventilated when using solvent-based products.

CARPET STAINS

Carpet cleaning solution contains 1 teaspoon mild detergent, 1 teaspoon white vinegar, and 1 quart warm water. Below are some tips for spots and stains:

- **Carefully blot or scrape the entire stained area** before applying any cleaning solution. Remove as much of the spill as possible. If you start cleaning too soon, you will make a bigger mess because the cleaning solution will spread the stain over more of the carpet.

- **Test the carpet** in an inconspicuous area making sure the cleaner does not damage or discolor carpet.

- **Do not rub a spill** for you may spread the problem to a larger area of carpeting. When you apply spot cleaner, work from the outside of the stain toward the inside to avoid spreading the stain.

- **After applying the cleaning solution**, blot up all the moisture in the carpeting. A clean white bath towel is best for drying carpet and brushing the nap back up to a standing position.

- **After blotting the carpet**, if you feel there is still too much moisture, place a ¾-thick stack of white towels over the spill and weight them with a heavy object or stand on the towels.

- **If the spot remover used alters the color** of the carpet, try touching up small places with artists' acrylic paint. If that doesn't work, try a felt-tip marker or a permanent-ink marker of the appropriate color. Go slowly, blending the colors into the fibers.

- **To raise depressions** left in carpet by heavy furniture, try steaming. Hold a steam iron close enough for steam to reach the carpet. Do not let the iron touch the fibers, especially if they are synthetic, because they could melt. Lift the fibers by scraping with the edge of a spoon.

REMOVING SPECIFIC STAINS FROM CARPETING

- **Blood**—Absorb as much of the blood as you can. Mix 1 teaspoon mild detergent, 1 teaspoon white vinegar, and 1 quart warm water. Apply the solution to the spot. Let the carpet dry. Apply a dry-cleaning fluid and let dry. Vacuum completely.

- **Butter**—First, scrape up as much butter as possible or absorb as much of melted butter as possible. Apply dry-cleaning fluid or Blue Dawn® in warm water. Rub lightly. Let the carpet dry. If the spot remains, reapply the fluid/Blue Dawn®. Dry thoroughly and vacuum.

- **Candle Wax**—The easiest way to remove candle wax from your carpet is to press an ice cube against the drip. The wax will harden and can then be pulled off. Treat any remaining traces of wax with dry-cleaning solution. Let the carpet dry and vacuum.

- **Candy**—Candy that contains no chocolate is easily removed from carpeting. Scrape up as much of the candy as possible. Mix 1 teaspoon mild detergent, 1 teaspoon white vinegar, and 1 quart warm water. Apply the solution to the spot. Let the carpet dry. If spot remains, reapply the solution. Let carpet dry and then vacuum.

- **Chewing Gum**—Chewing gum can be a very sticky mess. Press an ice cube against the blob of gum. The gum will harden and can then be pulled off. Treat any remaining traces of the chewing gum with dry-cleaning fluid. Let the carpet dry and vacuum.

- **Chocolate**—The longer chocolate stays on your carpet, the more difficult it is to remove. Scrape it from the carpet. Mix 1 teaspoon mild detergent, 1 teaspoon white vinegar, and 1 quart warm water. Apply the solution to the spot. Rinse with clear water, dry completely and vacuum gently.

- **Coffee**—Be sure to blot the coffee spill immediately. Using the same solution used for chocolate stains, apply the solution to the coffee stain. Let the carpet dry and then apply dry-cleaning fluid and let dry. Vacuum carpet completely.

- **Crayon**—For dropped crayons that have been stepped on and ground into the carpeting, scrape excess away and remove the rest by placing a blotter over the crayon stain and pressing it with a warm iron until the blotter absorbs the melted crayon. Move the blotter frequently so that it does not get oversaturated. Apply dry-cleaning fluid, and let the carpet dry. Reapply if necessary and then vacuum.

- **Fruit**—Fruit stains can be very hard to remove if they are allowed to set. But if you act quickly, the following method usually prevents a permanent stain. Scrape up spilled fruit and absorb fruit juice. Use the same solution mentioned under coffee and chocolate and apply to the spot. Let the carpet dry. If the spot remains, reapply the solution. Let the carpet dry and vacuum gently.

- **Ink**—Fast action is very essential when dealing with ink spots. Immediately apply dry-cleaning fluid. Let the carpet dry. If the spot remains, reapply the dry-cleaning fluid. Let the carpet dry thoroughly and vacuum.

- **Lipstick**—To remove lipstick, scrape away as much as possible. Apply dry-cleaning fluid and let dry. Then mix a solution of 1 teaspoon white vinegar, 1 teaspoon mild dishwater detergent, and 1 quart of warm water. Apply the solution to the spot. Let the carpet dry. If the spot remains, reapply the solution. Let the carpet dry and vacuum gently.

- **Milk**—Blot up the spilled milk. Apply the solution of detergent, vinegar, and water to the spilled area. Let the carpet dry and vacuum gently.

- **Mud**—Allow the mud tracked onto your carpet to dry. Brush or scrape off as much as possible. Use the carpet solution and apply to the spots. Let the carpet dry completely and then vacuum.

- **Nail Polish**—Apply dry-cleaning fluid, acetone, or polish remover to the spilled polish. Test the solvent you plan to use on an inconspicuous part of the carpet. Never apply solvents directly onto the carpet. If the stain remains, use carpet solution and apply to the spot. Let dry and then vacuum gently.

- **Soft Drinks**—The carbonation in drinks will help you clean spilled drinks quickly, but you must act fast. Some of the dyes found in drinks can stain your carpet permanently. Blot up the spilled drink. Using carpet solution, blot the spot thoroughly. Let the carpet dry. If spot remains, apply solution once again. Dry completely and vacuum gently.

- **Tea**—The tannic acid in tea is a potent dye, so move quickly when tea is spilled on your rug. Blot up the tea spill. Using carpet solution, apply to the spill. Let the carpet dry. Apply dry-cleaning fluid. Let the carpet dry and vacuum gently.

- **Urine**—Blot up urine immediately. Using carpet solution, apply to area. Let the carpet dry and vacuum gently.

- **Vomit**—Treat immediately. Blot up as much as possible, then dilute immediately with baking soda and water or club soda. Apply a solution of ammonia (1 part) and water (10 parts). Rinse with cold water. Let dry, and then vacuum.

Note: Dry-cleaning solution called for in many stain cleaning instructions can be found at local hardware stores.

AGE-APPROPRIATE
Chores for Kids [12]

A FAMILY IS A TEAM:

Everyone shares in the responsibility of keeping the home. Children are never too young to learn to help. Both my girls taught their children at a young age to fold washcloths and from there proceeded to bigger items. If you start at a young age giving them simple responsibilities, helping around the house will become natural to them.

2-4 year old

- Help dust
- Put napkins on table
- Help put away toys
- Put laundry in hamper
- Help feed pet

4-7 year old

"Help" is the important word at this age. Many of the chores will be done as a helper and slowly kids can graduate to doing them independently.

- Set the table or help set the table
- Put away toys/things
- Help feed pets
- Water plants
- Help make bed
- Dust
- Put laundry in hamper
- Help put dishes in dishwasher
- Water the garden
- Help wipe up messes
- Help with yard work (rake with child's rake or plant flowers, etc.)
- Help clear table
- Help put away groceries

[12] Age-Appropriate Chores for Kids]: "Free Printable Behavior Charts." www.freeprintablebehaviorcharts.com.

8-10 year old

- Make bed
- Water plants
- Clean room with direction
- Set the table
- Clear the table
- Dust
- Vacuum
- Feed pets
- Help make dinner
- Put laundry in hamper
- Help wash the car
- Help wash dishes
- Help load/empty dishwasher
- Rake leaves
- Take out the trash

---

11 year old and older

- Take out garbage
- Set the table
- Clear the table
- Clean room with direction
- Put away groceries
- Clean the bathroom with direction
- Clean the kitchen
- Dust
- Vacuum
- Mow lawn
- Feed pets
- Water plants
- Put laundry in hamper
- Help with laundry and eventually start doing own laundry
- Help make dinner/make small meals on own
- Help wash the car/wash car
- Make bed
- Help with yard work
- Shovel snow
- Wash dishes/load or empty dishwasher

ESTHER
A Woman for Such a Time as This

Biblical Principle: God uses women with a willing heart to accomplish His divine purposes.

Read the book of Esther.

1. Who was Esther? How was she described?

2. Whose care was she placed in within the king's palace?

3. What was Mordecai's relationship to Esther and what were his instructions to her once she was inside the king's palace?

4. What did Esther ask of Mordecai and her people?

5. Did God answer their prayers and fasting? How? Have you developed the discipline of fasting in your Christian life? Why or why not?

6. Why did Esther go before the king? Do you believe God had Esther in King Ahasuerus' palace for a specific reason? What was it?

7. Who was an enemy of Esther, the Jewish people, and Mordecai? What did he desire to do to them?

8. How did Mordecai end up the *hero*?

9. How is Esther rewarded for her obedience to God?

Through Esther's willingness to answer God's call, she saved her people. God placed her within the king's palace *for such a time as this*. Be mindful when God has a desire and a plan to use you for *such a time as this*.

Week Six Notes

What I Learned Today

Week Seven

DECORATING MADE SIMPLE

Introduction
EFFICIENCY DÉCOR

*S*ome friends and I were at lunch one day reminiscing about our first year of marriage and our very first apartment. Everyone agreed that some of their fondest memories were those spent in their first apartment as newlyweds. On the way home that day, I began to think about our first place. Mark found it, and he was so proud. I hadn't seen it prior to our wedding because I lived in Nashville, and our home-to-be was in south Florida. We flew to Florida the morning after our wedding. Once we arrived, we retrieved our luggage, picked up the car, and set out for our new home, an *efficiency* apartment. Perhaps you are like me; I had no clue what an *efficiency* apartment was! As we pulled up the short drive, I noticed that there were two front doors rather close to one another. I asked if this was a duplex. Mark answered, "Not quite."

He unlocked the door and welcomed me into our new home. Let me give you a quick tour. I say quick because I discovered that an *efficiency* apartment is one-quarter of a small house! I stepped into the living room to see our bed/couch (living room and bedroom all in one), the only closet, the bathroom, the kitchenette, and the back door all at once. I told you it would be a quick tour! How clever of someone to design the living room that instantly makes into a bedroom just by removing the rectangular back cushions of the couch! It must have been a man who designed it so he could watch TV in bed. To say I was shocked would be an understatement. Now, I wasn't expecting a mansion for after all we were a young married couple.

We were in south Florida to work and save money for graduate school, not to live in luxury—but an *efficiency* apartment? Needless to say, the decorating took very little time or effort. The only furniture we had was two plastic parson's tables. I know, what is a parson's table? Here it is: a plastic square top in which is stored the four plastic legs. When removed and pushed into the compartments in each of the four corners underneath, you instantly have a coffee table with four chunky legs that stands about twenty-four inches high. Wow! Of course I had to decorate the tops of our cute chunky white plastic coffee tables, so I purchased a glass globe that sat atop a wood base and was filled with red and gold *dried* flowers—the flowers of the 1970s. All matched perfectly with our black and cream coverlet that was provided over our bed/couch—not at all what I would choose now!

---

*Y*our taste, like mine, will change over the years, but I want to encourage you to step out and trust yourself to know what you like and what you don't like in color, fabric, furniture styles, etc. Establish an apartment or home that reflects you, not your parents! If you feel insecure in this area and don't have a natural eye for decorating, find a friend or acquaintance who does.

Whatever your living quarters, know that it is your home, and you need to make it feel like home and reflect you as a person. You don't have to break the bank to accomplish this! Shop smart and when choosing colors, choose what you like. When choosing furniture, choose what you can afford, the fabric you like, and something that is comfortable. Home sweet home does not have to look like a showroom at a furniture store. It just needs to be warm and inviting!

REFLECTING YOUR STYLE

She makes for herself coverlets, cushions, and rugs of tapestry. Her clothing is linen, pure and fine, and purple (wool). Give her of the product of her hands, And let her own works praise her in the gates (of the city).

Proverbs 31:22, 31 AMP

Your home needs to reflect your life style, your taste, and your heart. When beginning the decorating process, here are some do's and don'ts ...

DON'T...

- **Compare your home or apartment** to the homes of friends, family, or acquaintances. If you are married this can harm your spouse's self-esteem; he will feel that he does not sufficiently provide for you and your family. If you are single, this will rob you of contentment.

- **Copy someone else's taste in design.** You can repeat an occasional decorative idea, but be yourself—do your own thing! You live in your home, let it be a reflection of you.

- **Go into debt in order to have a full house**—full of furniture and fully decorated. The old adage is true, "good things come to those who wait." A full house can cause an empty bank account!

- **Buy sales items** that do not complete or compliment your décor just because they are a "good deal." Coming home with a lamp or an accessory thinking that you will find a place to display it is a waste of money that could have been spent on a more beneficial decorative item to complete or compliment your design.

- **Be discontent** with what you have—discontentment reflects an ungrateful heart!

- **Be impatient** by wanting everything immediately. If you get all you want or feel you must have as soon as you move into your home, you will be so far in debt that you cannot enjoy your home. Moving onto the next "want" on your list and going into debt because of it will not bring you peace or joy.

DO...

- **Set a budget!** Do not exceed your determined budget.

- **Make a list of items** you need to complete the decorating of the room you are working on and stick to your list.

- **Pray**—I pray before I go shop, and it is amazing how many times the Lord leads me to a good deal, one that fits my budget. He knows what is best for me and what I can afford.

- **Shop smart!** Save your money in order to buy better quality furniture—it will last for years!

- **Be content!** Discontentment breeds discontentment, robbing you of joy and peace. God will not honor an ungrateful, discontented heart. Contentment brings peace and joy!

- **Be patient**—You will better appreciate those things you were willing to wait for.

- **Be yourself**—God made you with your own unique taste; trust what you like.

Proverbs 31:27a says, "She looks well to how things go in her household." AMP

RESOURCES FOR DECORATING

MAGAZINES

- Architectural Digest
- Better Homes and Gardens
- Bridge for Design
- Country Home
- Country Living
- Do It Yourself
- Family Handyman
- Flea Market Décor
- House Beautiful
- Interior Design
- Martha Stewart Living
- Real Simple
- Southern Living
- Taste of Home
- This Old House
- Traditional Home

CATALOGS

- Ballard Designs
- Crate and Barrel
- Frontgate
- Garnet Hill (Bedding)
- Horshow
- Pottery Barn

HOME DECORATING [13]

Taunton House Decorating Book by Heather J. Paper

Creating comfortable living quarters is more than a matter of shopping for a new piece of furniture. Whether you are starting from scratch or simply doing a little redecorating, it's important to first take a look at the big picture. Determine whether your family members live formally or if they are more laid back. Take a look at the colors and styles you like most. Be sure to figure kids and pets into the equation.

PERSONAL STYLE

The way you like to live will have a strong influence on the way you decorate your home. Are you more relaxed in a traditional setting, with wingback chairs and a camelback sofa? Or are you the type who likes the sleek contemporary style? If you are unsure, try this simple exercise: thumb through several decorating books looking for rooms that you find appealing; there will be some common decorating threads among them that will give you a sense of where to start. You may even find that you like elements of different styles, putting you in the eclectic category.

COLOR CUES

The choice of color palettes is purely personal. Similar to furniture styles, colors can speak volumes about your individual tastes. Pick up a stack of paint chips and you will see why choosing a palette can seem like an insurmountable task. In order to make the decision easier, here are a few clues. We all have a favorite color, so start by simply considering the various tints and shades within the color family you like. Also, think about the room and how it will be used. Is it a living room where you will entertain often? If so, consider neutral hues that will make most guests comfortable. The biggest clue is your wardrobe. Take a look at the colors you wear each day. Chances are if you are comfortable wearing them, you will be comfortable living with them.

A SMOOTH BLEND

In the process of decorating a room it is possible to spend too many hours trying to match colors. In fact, that is not necessary or desirable. It is more important that colors blend. For example, if you have two or three blues within a room, they will be right at home together if they are of similar tones and intensities. If you are uncertain if your colors will work together, try this simple test: gather the colors together, step back, and look at them through squinted eyes. If they seem to become a single shade, then you have a beautiful blend of colors.

HARMONY

It is imperative that there be at least one or two common threads of color. You can use multiple patterns within a room as long as you can connect them somehow, and they are in harmony.

[13] Heather J. Paper, Home Decorating (Taunton Press, 2005).

THE FAMILY ROOM

Creating a successful arrangement in the family room may be the easiest of all. Simply start with your largest seating piece—the sofa—and orient it toward the room's focal point, typically the home-entertainment center (the television). More often than not, this multipurpose storage piece is placed against the largest wall. Complete the seating group, making sure that each piece of furniture is no more than eight to ten feet apart, for easy conversation. Because you should be able to view the television without craning your neck, swivel chairs are often a good solution. Also, keep in mind that this is often where casual meals are served. Sit in each seat, making sure that there's a nearby place to sit a glass or dish. If not, you will need to add a small table or two.

LIVING ROOM

There is no hard and fast rule in terms of room arrangements, even in the living room. But a few guidelines will help you create a comfortable and inviting atmosphere. When placing your main seating pieces, keep in mind that people are most at ease sitting across from each other or at tight right angles. It is hard to converse if you are sitting too closely together side by side; even if your sofa can easily accommodate four people, plan on seating no more than three. For additional seating, use benches, ottomans, and nearby dining room chairs. Small upholstered cubes are a good choice as well. When not in use they can tuck away under a console table. Some cocktail tables come with cubes that nest underneath the tabletop until they are needed. Once you have lived with your furniture plan for a while, reassess how it is working. If it feels like you have too much furniture, don't hesitate to move a piece or two to another room. It is all a part of finding the right comfort level.

SCALE

Simply put, scale refers to the relationship among furnishings within a room. Visual weight as well as size comes into play. Many people flank a sofa with two end tables. If you don't want a matched set (in this age of eclecticism, that's the case more often than not), be sure that your selections are compatible in scale, with each other as well as with the sofa between them. For one end of a plush sofa, you might choose a set of nesting tables two inches taller than the sofa's arm; on the other end, you may opt for a small chest that's two inches lower. They both work with the height of the sofa and from a visual point of view too. The multiple legs of the nesting tables balance the mass of the chest at the opposite end.

WALL ART

We are long past the day when wall art consisted solely of paintings, posters, and prints. Today, we are more inclined to let our imaginations run wild, hanging anything that can be supported by a nail in the wall. From decorative plates to architectural elements—even store signs, boat oars, or a crisscross pair of skis—wall art is truly in the eye of the beholder. What if the objects of your desire are not conducive to being hung on a wall? There is often a way around that; small items such as pottery and figurines fit neatly on wall-hung shelves.

ARRANGING FURNITURE

Arranging furniture is one of the most daunting—yet most important—design decision you can make. These common scenarios will teach you the basics of furniture placement.

- Whether your room is big or small, having the right furniture arrangement will make it more enjoyable. Knowing how to arrange furniture can help you navigate how a room will be used.

- When arranging living room furniture; leave room for traffic and an entry drop spot.

- The living room furniture arrangement should provide for visiting guests, but still feel cozy when it's only you and your family.

- Cozy key seating pieces up to the fireplace facing each other. Arranging furniture around a fireplace, especially in the winter, makes your living room feel inviting.

- Use end tables as landing spaces on both ends of the sofa.

- Pair chairs to balance the visual weight of the sofa and to maximize seating.

- If you have no free walls and a centered fireplace, float seating in the center of a room filled with doors and windows.

- Face chairs and sofa toward each other to encourage conversation. Anchor the conversation grouping with a rug and a large coffee table.

- Frame the space with additional seating and cabinets for storage positioned around the perimeter of the room along the walls.

- If you're not sure how to arrange furniture in a living room, orient seating so it takes advantage of whatever view your room has to offer, whether it's a TV or a bank of windows. Create your own focal point by hanging a large piece of art on a wall or create a vignette of favorite objects on a console or bookshelf. If you can't decide between arranging the furniture around the fireplace or the TV, choose both and mount the TV above the fireplace.

- For face-to-face conversations, place seating no more than 8 feet apart. In a large living room, use furniture to create comfortable islands. Face two sofas in the center of a room, and place a group of chairs and side tables at one end to create a separate conversation area. A furniture arrangement that encourages conversation is the best kind for making memories in your home.

- Leaving enough space between pieces is vital in arranging furniture. Allow 30 inches between furniture you need to be able to walk around and 14 to 18 inches between a coffee table and sofa, so drinks are within reaching distance. This should still be held true when planning a large living room furniture arrangement. If a piece of furniture is too far away, it may look like it's floating in the room without purpose.

- The key to a good furniture arrangement is all in the details—especially side tables and coffee tables. Consider your room size and furniture arrangement when choosing the right coffee table. Use round pedestal tables as side tables between chairs and sofas. The curves of round tables make them easier to navigate around. When space is tight, use nesting tables for flexible use when needed.

- In an irregular room with one wide traffic lane, use the perimeter of the room for a computer desk and storage console. Choose chairs with casters so that they are easy to move. Float the furniture to focus on the fireplace and the television. Ensure that the living room furniture is arranged near both the fireplace and television.

- Always place the television so the screen faces away from the sunlight. The viewing distance for a standard TV is 8 to 12 feet, and the best viewing angle is not more than 30 degrees. For traffic flow, create paths that flow behind viewers and not between them and the screen.

- Family rooms can oftentimes be storage hubs, so a good living room furniture arrangement makes room for cabinets, drop zones, and drawers. Consider freestanding pieces in a smaller room and wall-to-wall built-ins in a larger room. Always allow for some storage near the TV for media items.

- Lighting is a key factor in the overall mood of your room and plays a big part when planning how to arrange living room furniture. Windows let in ample natural light, while chandeliers, sconces, and lamps keep the room bright at night. Improve lighting by installing in-floor electrical outlets to service floating furniture arrangements.

EFFECTIVE LIGHTING for Your Home [14]

How you light your home is an important part of decorating. Lighting interior design contributes greatly to the look and feel of a room. There are many types of lighting that can be used in various rooms.

- **Ambient or General Lighting**—Illuminates the whole room. Recessed and track lighting are the most popular. Certain wall sconces are another example. It is recommended that you install a dimmer switch with your track and recessed light so that you have the added flexibility in adjusting the brightness.

- **Task Lighting**—Provides sufficient light to help you perform the task at hand, reading, cooking, shaving, etc. Task lighting should be glare free, and it should make things easy to see without tiring or straining your eyes.

- **Accent Lighting**—This light is focused lighting that is used to illuminate a sculpture, piece of art, or architectural element in a room. Accent lighting is about three times as bright as ambient lighting.

- **Natural Light**—This light comes through windows, doors, and skylights. Depending on the time of day, season, or weather, it can vary in brightness and intensity. Rooms can be arranged to take advantage of the position of the sun at different times of day. This type of lighting is also called kinetic lighting because the light from outside moves. It is one of the less reliable types, as it is affected by the seasons and the weather, but natural lighting can produce an effect unequaled by any artificial light source, when used properly.

Do not be afraid to use multiple types of interior lighting in a room. In fact, this is highly desirable and will create very dramatic effects. Using several strategies at once in a room allows you to turn any light off, changing the look and feel with the flick of a switch. This can be effective for creating different moods in different rooms at night.

- Lighting can also be effective in making a room look larger or smaller. Example: If a room seems too narrow, then wash one wall with light to visually expand it.

- If a ceiling is high, but you want the room to have a cozier and intimate feel, do not allow much light to escape beyond the height of the light/lamp shade. Try up-lighting the ceiling to make a room appear larger.

You will find hundreds of home lighting options for your home. Think of lighting from two aspects *functional and aesthetic.* Functionally, home lighting needs to provide the correct type of light in sufficient quantity for the intended purpose. Aesthetically, it can be configured to create the desired mood through intensity and color.

[14] "Effective Ways to Use Lighting In Interior Design." www.home-decorating-made-easy.com/home-lighting.html

Lighting in Rooms

LIVING ROOM

1. Place a lamp behind every reader's shoulder, about twenty-four inches above the floor.

2. Highlight a framed piece of art with halogen track lighting or by attaching a picture light.

3. Use accent lights to illuminate book or display shelves.

4. Install recessed lighting as your general lighting or to bring out beautiful wall textures.

5. Use dimmer switches to change lighting atmosphere.

DINING ROOM

1. A chandelier over a table sets a beautiful setting.

2. Highlight a framed piece of art with halogen track lighting or by attaching a picture light.

3. Install halogen strip lighting in your china cabinet to highlight china or collectibles.

4. If a chandelier is not your taste and you have a long table, try a trio of pendant lights.

BEDROOM

1. Place table lamps on your bedside tables. For children's rooms, avoid halogen lamps, which get very hot.

2. Wall sconces can provide good general lighting without being too bright.

3. If there is not much space, consider recessed lights or pendant lights.

4. Don't forget candlelight if a romantic setting is what you have in mind.

Candice Olson, celebrated interior designer and one-time TV host, said, "The most important part of any decorating project is lighting." According to Olson, without it, décor falls short of the sparkle factor and then the project budget is wasted. [15]

PROPER WAYS TO HANG PICTURES
and Display Artwork

STEP ONE:

Measure the distance between the wire at full tension and the top of the frame.

STEP TWO:

Measure the height of your frame and divide the result in half.

STEP THREE:

From the floor, measure up the wall to fifty-eight inches and make a light pencil mark.

STEP FOUR:

From the pencil mark, measure upward the distance recorded in step 2 and make a second light pencil mark.

STEP FIVE:

From this pencil mark, measure downward the distance recorded in step 1.

STEP SIX:

Place nail and hanger here.

BASICS ON HANGING PICTURES AND WALL ART

An arrangement of favorite framed photographs, wall art, or collectibles can add personality and warmth to any room. When done correctly, wall art can change the focal point or the entire look of any room.

- **Pictures should hang just above eye level.** Eye level is often defined as art center aligned at fifty-eight inches from the floor. While this is a good guideline for larger pieces, it can leave smaller pieces stranded on a wall. It is acceptable to hang a small print at seated eye level, so that the seated person can enjoy the view.

- **If most of the time people are standing in the room**, then the eye level should be directed at the viewers who are standing. In a room where the viewers will spend the majority of the time seated, like a living room, eye level would be from a seated position.

- **Creating a group of art or photos on a wall** is an excellent way to create an interesting focal point. This task, however, requires extra planning. It is suggested that you map out the way you would like to arrange your pictures on the floor first. This way, you can move them around without leaving holes in the wall.

- **The secret to arranging art on the wall is simple ...** balance, balance, balance! Use a measuring tape to be sure that the distance between several pictures that will hang in a row is equal. Four small pictures on the left can be balanced with two medium-sized pictures on the right. Be patient, take your time, measure, and plan.

- **Consider lighting to emphasize your arrangement.** When lighting is directed to the arrangement, it commands even more attention. This type of lighting should be subdued and not cause a glare. Be careful of lighting that is too bright.

- **Add diversity to the arrangement.** Use frames and mats that are different sizes and shapes, but complement one another.

- **Pay attention to balance in your entire room.** Be careful not to put everything in one part of the room. Leaving the other walls bare will throw the balance of the entire room off.

ARRANGING ART GROUPINGS:

- **Working horizontally**, as on a sofa wall or hall entrance—Prints grouped in odd numbers are visually balanced, giving volume without crowding.

- **Even number arrangements**—Large spaces: Tightly group an even number of pictures to balance a large space, such as a high wall in a room with vaulted ceilings. Small spaces: Tightly group an even number of pictures in a small space, such as a gallery kitchen or a tight stair landing, to give a window effect. Enhance the effect by using light colors and slender frames. In both cases, the trick to evenly numbered collections is tight grouping so that pieces appear as one statement rather than a series of small comments.

- **Symmetrical art placement**—If you have a selection of pictures that are similar in subject matter, size, and framing consider a symmetrical grouping to create a mirror-image balance. Symmetrical collections are often used to create the popular gallery effects, above large pieces of furniture, such as sofas and above mantles.

- **Asymmetrical wall arrangements**—If you have a selection of dissimilar pictures with at least one common element, such as subject matter, use an asymmetrical grouping for balance. When hanging two larger pictures together, try lowering one and raising the other so that the top and bottom do not match. Group larger and smaller pieces to create interest and energy. Example: Hang a large focal piece, such as a garden scene, with two smaller pieces, such as gardening tools or seed packets. Combine horizontal and vertical pieces in the same grouping. Hang a tall architectural print with two panoramic skyline photos.

- **Spacing pictures**—Tightly spaced is two inches or less between prints. Normal spacing is four to six inches apart. Trick to use: place your hand with fingers closed between the prints.

BASIC GROUPINGS OF ART WITH FURNITURE:

- **Fill two-thirds of the wall space**—When placing art above furniture such as sofas, chair groupings, or console tables, eyeball the amount of space between the furniture and the ceiling, and then allocate two-thirds of that space for pictures.

- **How high to hang**—Hanging a picture too high above a piece of furniture can leave both pieces feeling disconnected. A good guideline is five to nine inches above the furniture.

- **Spacing art**—When hanging a print above a sofa, remember to leave arm space above the sofa back.

- **Pictures and oversized furniture**—Oversized furniture calls for robust prints to strike a balance. For visual weight, consider a grouping of two to three prints that carry strong visual weight through color or wider molding and mat combination.

EFFECTIVE BOOKCASING *for Your Home*

- Less is more these days, so do not overload your bookshelves.

- Mix antique books and accessories with new coffee table books of interest.

- Stand up pretty porcelain plates, toile trays, and framed antique drawings on top of books and position them in between vertical stacks of books.

- Create a zigzag pattern of large objects and colorful books from upper shelf to lower shelf, to keep the eye interested and moving from top to bottom.

- Vary the texture of items on the shelves. Mix woven baskets, painted wooden folk art, metal and wooden boxes, and framed art work among shinier porcelain items to enliven the shelves.

- Think large scale when choosing bookshelf accessories and books. Coffee table books that are too large can be stacked horizontally to fit. A single large inexpensive basket has more impact than an expensive collection of miniatures. Save the miniatures for a small tabletop where they can be stars in their own right.

- Consider painting or wallpapering the back wall of your bookcases a fun pattern, deeper tone, or a contrasting color to make the accessories pop visually.

- Tuck a small pot of ivy into an interesting cachepot, box, or basket and place into your shelf arrangement.

- If space allows, consider placing a small lamp on a shelf. It adds warmth to the room.

PAINTING 101 [16]

Be sure to choose the proper type of paint for the job. The two major types of interior paint are latex, which is water-based and can be cleaned up with soap and water, and alkyd, which is oil-based and must be cleaned with paint thinner. Latex is the easiest to use.

Paints come in four finishes with varying degrees of shine: flat, satin, semi-gloss, and gloss:

- **Flat**—No sheen; best on walls in low-use areas, like dining rooms, living rooms, and bedrooms; washable but not scrubable.

- **Satin**—Slight sheen; good for walls and trim in higher use areas like hallways and kids rooms; washable and scrubable. This is the most popular sheen; it is durable and elegant.

- **Semi-gloss**—Medium sheen; good for walls and trim in high abuse areas like kitchens, bathrooms, laundry rooms; washable and scrubable.

- **Gloss**—High sheen; best for trim and cabinets; washable and scrubable.

When painting the walls and trim, use lower sheen on the walls and a higher sheen on the trim.

OIL-BASED PAINT:

Commonly used on molding, cabinets, and furniture. It provides a protective coating and creates a smoother finish than water-based paint.

Advantages of Oil:

- Goes on smoother
- Covers more thoroughly in one coat
- Shrinks less
- Takes longer to dry so you have more working time
- Holds up well in high-traffic areas

Disadvantages of Oil:

- More likely to crack, fade, and yellow over time
- Fumes can be overwhelming
- Clean-up solvents like mineral spirits and turpentine are necessary for cleaning brushes. These hazardous chemicals need to be managed carefully.

OTHER IMPORTANT CONSIDERATIONS:

- Oil-based paints should never be poured down a drain.

- Many cities have a local hazardous waste collection center that accepts old paint and stain. No matter which formula you reach for, oil or latex, use a laundry or bath sink for minor clean-up. Paint can ruin kitchen disposals.

---

[16] "Paint Glossary: All About Paint, Color, and Tools: Home Improvement: Home and Garden." www.hgtv.com/interior painting.

LATEX:

Often called acrylic latex because it contains a plastic resin made of acrylics or polyvinyl, which adheres better.

Advantages of Latex:

- Doesn't yellow over time
- Environmentally friendly
- Dries faster
- Much easier to clean up by using soap and water
- Latex is far more forgiving, primarily for cleanup, making it a great choice for the weekend warrior
- Many painters are finding latex is more widely available than oil
- Disadvantage of latex: it swells the grain of wood, making sanding between coats a necessity

More Painting Tips:

- All paints contain chemicals, so wear gloves when tackling large projects to minimize direct skin exposure.
- If you're painting a wall or doing some simple effects, reach for latex. If there's wood involved, you may want to consider oil-based paint.
- When in doubt, tell the experts at your local paint/hardware store what you're doing and they'll be happy to offer advice.

ALL ABOUT PAINT:

To tell if your current wall color is water-based or oil-based, douse a white cloth with rubbing alcohol and rub it on the wall (in an out-of-the-way spot). If the paint softens and begins to transfer onto the cloth, it is water based. If the alcohol does not remove any color, it is oil-based.

- **Primer**—Used to seal bare surfaces and provide a base for paint to grab on to. If you have spackled your walls, priming is a must to keep spackling from bleeding through the paint. Use water-based primer on new drywall, previously painted walls (including those that have been patched, repaired or stained), galvanized metal, and non-ferrous metals. Use oil-based primer on severely stained or damaged walls, on paneling, under wallpaper, and on wrought iron, ferrous metal, and raw wood.

- **Sheen**—Paint's sheen gives it a certain finish and quality. There are several options: matte-flat, eggshell, and satin.

- **Matte-Flat**—Smooth finish has little or no sheen. Helps hide surface imperfections but may suffer damage more easily than other finishes. Best for low-traffic areas.

- **Eggshell**—Velvety sheen, easy to clean. Great middle-of-the-road option between flat and high gloss. Gives a flatter look than glossy paint but still provides hard-wearing and protective coating.

- **Satin**—Silky, pearl-like finish, stain resistant. Creates protective shell that resists moisture and mildew. Good for kitchens, bathrooms, and high-traffic areas.

- **Semi-Gloss**—Sleek, radiant, and high resistance to moisture. Good for cabinets, doors, and windows.

- **High Gloss**—Very durable and easy to clean. It's a glass-like finish and is good for trim and molding.

- **Water-Based Paint**—Latex paint is often called water-based, commonly used on walls and ceilings; it is less toxic and easier to clean up than the oil-based paints. Water-based paint comes in a variety of sheens including matte, eggshell, or high gloss. It is a paint that works well on surfaces previously painted with latex or flat oil-based paints. It usually doesn't adhere well to high-gloss finishes and cannot be used on bare steel because it will rust it. Water-based paint can be used on top of wallpaper, but there is a risk that the water in the paint may cause the paper to peel away from the wall.

TOOLS:

- **Paintbrushes**—Which is best? Use a nylon-bristle brush for water-based paint and natural bristles for oil-based paint. Do not use natural bristles with water-based paint; the water can make the bristles limp. Foam brushes are good for intricate work such as painting molding or window casings. These brushes usually last for only one use because they're hard to clean and easy to tear.

- **Paintbrush Shape**: Angled-sash Paintbrush—The bristles are shaped at an angle to make it easier to cut into corners and paint moldings. And, Straight-end paint brushes—The bristles are cut at the same length.

- **Types of Bristles**—The best brushes have bristles that are flagged and tipped. Flagged bristles are slightly split, so they'll hold more paint and spread it more smoothly. Tipped bristles are slightly tapered to help release an even, controllable amount of paint. Typically, the more expensive the brush, the easier the paint job!

CLEANING PAINTBRUSHES:

For latex paint, use soap and water to clean paint from the brush immediately after painting. If the painting dries on the brush, you'll need special solvents to remove it. If your house is on a public sewer system, you can clean the brushes in your sink, but be careful not to dispose of paint in an area where it might seep into the groundwater.

For oil-based paints, you'll need a solvent such as paint thinner or mineral spirits. Pour about two inches of thinner into a metal container and swirl the dirty brush in, until the paint comes off. Press the brush against the side of the container to remove excess thinner and clean off the remaining thinner with the rag, then rinse with soap and water. If oil-based paint dries on your brush, soak it in paint thinner for a few minutes before cleaning. Most paint brushes can be wrapped in plastic wrap or original covering.

Hang brushes with bristles down to maintain their shape.

PAINTING PADS:

These can be very useful for cutting around trim. The pads come with small wheels that allow you to paint up to the edge of the trim without getting paint on the trim.

ROLLER COVERS

Paint rollers are time savers on any paint project. Using the correct roller cover can make your painting a lot smoother.

- **Nap**—The correct nap length of roller cover all depends on the texture of the surface to be painted. For a rough surface, use a roller with a long nap length. For smooth surfaces, use a shorter nap length.

- **Fiber**—Mohair is good for applying enamel paint. Lamb's wool covers are excellent for alkyd paints, but not for latex. Synthetic fibers are the most versatile but cannot be used with epoxies and polyurethane.

- **Core**—Cardboard cores are not very durable because they absorb the paint; they get soft and often lose their shape. Typically, the greater the cost the higher the quality.

ROLLER COVERS

- **For latex paint**, scrape as much paint off the roller as possible. Partially fill a sink or large bucket with warm water and roll the applicator back and forth. If necessary, use detergent with the water to remove difficult paint. Rinse the roller until the water is clear. Let dry. Once dry, rollers can be stored in a clean plastic zipper-lock bag for future use within the week.

- **For oil-based paint**, scrape as much paint as possible off the roller. Roll the applicator in a paint tray containing mineral spirits or paint thinner then wash the roller in soapy water. Rinse thoroughly and let dry. If doing a job over two to four days, you can wrap the brush/roller in cellophane, place in a plastic zipper-lock bag, and store in the refrigerator between jobs. With oil-based paint jobs, the brushes used can also be wrapped in plastic wrap, placed in a plastic zipper-lock bag, and stored in the refrigerator overnight. If paint is collecting in the bristles of the brush to the point of affecting the look of the paint job, clean and let dry. It is always good to have at least two identical brushes on an oil-based paint job, in order to have one drying while using the other. If the paint begins to collect gobs of paint and cause difficulty in painting, go ahead and clean the brush thoroughly.

- **No-hassle paint touch-ups**: Instead of getting the roller out to do a touch up, take an old washcloth, dip it in the paint can and bounce it over the spot a few times. The washcloth leaves the same kind of texture as a roller sleeve and you can throw it away when you are done.

MARY
A Woman of Honor

Biblical Principle: A woman fully submitted to God's will for her life is a woman to be honored.

Read Luke 1:26–56, Matthew 1:18–24, Luke 2:1–20, and Luke 2:21–40.

1. Who was sent by God to Mary and what news did he have for her?

2. How did Gabriel address Mary?

3. What was her response?

4. If you had been Mary, knowing the culture she was living in and the shame that came with being pregnant outside of wedlock, what would your response have been? Is your whole being yielded to God as Mary's was?

5. Through her song, we see Mary worshipping her Savior and we see her rejoicing in what He had asked of her. It is obvious from her words of expression that she knew God's Word. Is it evident to those around you that worship is a key part of your life? Is it evident that you know the Word? Is it evident that you have hidden it within your heart?

6. Mary was attentive to God's voice. Are you?

7. Mary submitted to God's will for her life. Will you?

8. Mary trusted God. Do you?

9. Mary was a woman of godly character. Are you?

10. Mary was a woman who knew God's Word and believed it. Do you?

11. Mary was willing to bear shame, humiliation, and public ridicule in order to fulfill God's purpose and plan for her life. Are you?

12. Mary was a woman of honor, chosen by God to carry His son. She was a woman that we as women should look up to and study, so that we can emulate her life. What have you learned from Mary?

Week Seven Notes

What I Learned Today

Week Eight

TIPS ON GARDENING, FLOWERS, AND CANNING

Introduction

BLACKBERRY PICKIN'

Now that I'm older, I find myself reflecting back on my childhood experiences and memories. Ones that vividly stand out are the summers spent with my grandparents—hours from home and family. I remember the summer in Ohio when I went to church camp with them. My Grandpa decided that I needed to attend the children's church service. He was determined I was going to go. I set out from our little cabin to cross this incredibly huge campground; well, it seemed huge to a little five-year-old girl. I went reluctantly, but not far! I hid behind the first tree I came to, thinking he and Grandma wouldn't see me. But they did see me, and Grandpa was not happy with my disobedience. I could be a fairly hard-headed little one! His solution to my refusal to go and my outright disobedience was a good old-fashioned spanking! In fact, it was the only time my Grandpa spanked me. But I went!

I also remember the summer in Springfield, Ohio following my third-grade year. What a fun summer! Grandma and Grandpa had planted a garden in their backyard. I can still smell the bright colored marigolds planted around the edge of the garden, supposedly to keep critters out. My grandparents were very meticulous people. I remember their freezer and how detailed and orderly it was. In fact, Grandpa had placed a diagram on the inside of the lid displaying where each item was located. Looking into the freezer, many items were wrapped neatly in freezer paper and secured with freezer tape. Others were placed in clear freezer containers, stacked, and labeled with his beautifully neat handwriting, something I did not inherit! It was a work of art. That summer, I spent hours either on the screened-in porch or in the basement playing with a wicker picnic basket, complete with four colorful place settings of plastic dishes—silverware, napkins, and all.

Evansville, Indiana, was the summer of my seventh-grade year. Grandpa hadn't been the pastor very long at Evansville First Church, so we hadn't been in the city previous to my stay. My Grandma was working part time at Sears, so Grandpa would come home and cook hamburgers for the two of us at lunchtime. He was a great cook and a sweet man. I cherish those lunches with him.

One Sunday, Grandpa suggested we go blackberry picking. Now, keep in mind, it was the middle of the summer. I am, and was as a child, very hot natured. We set out into the woods that hot Sunday afternoon to find blackberries, and to say I had an attitude from the onset would be putting it mildly. I was HOT and determined to make their lives and our blackberry pickin' time miserable! Looking back, I can see that I missed an opportunity to make a great memory with my grandparents, but then what do we know at thirteen? A little sweating, a little itching, and a few thorns was a small price to pay for a sweet memory! While living in Evansville, a member of the church had given them a parcel of land in which to plant a garden. I remember picking corn and digging up potatoes and carrots. That was also the year Grandpa planted Big Boy tomatoes along the back side of his garage and decided to use a new product on the market called Miracle Grow—talk about BIG BOYS! Those were the biggest tomatoes I had ever seen.

I have many fond memories of my grandparents, the summers spent with them and their many gardens. You too can make memories for your family gardening together!

Grow, Grow, Grow a Garden

According to an article in *Home Life Magazine*,[17] many American families are growing their own fresh fruits and vegetables to save money and avoid pesticides. Below are seven steps to growing your own garden:

1. Plan the place. Choose a central location easily accessible.

2. Find level ground that gets plenty of light and has good drainage (slopes down).

3. Begin by creating 4'x10' plots—as many as you desire in order to grow your garden.

4. Pick your plants. Consult the *Farmer's Almanac* or *Rodale's All-New Encyclopedia of Organic Gardening* for charts listing crops, their yields, and planting times. Some good choices are nutrient-rich vegetables: asparagus, garden beans, broccoli, beets, peppers, parsley, basil, lettuce, squash, cabbage, and strawberries.

5. Plant your crops. Drop seeds into trenches, and set seedlings in generous holes, allowing space for their roots. Be sure to water as you go, and label each plant or row.

6. Maintain growth. Take a half hour every few days to weed and water.

7. Harvest the bounty. Harvest promptly and regularly or plants will quit producing. Share the fruits of your labor!

Your Local Farmers' Market

If gardening is not your thing but you desire to eat healthy, go visit your local farmers' market or locate a farm like the Jones Valley Urban Farm., a community-based nonprofit organic farm, located in Birmingham, Alabama. The executive director, at the farm says, "I don't think there is any way that anyone could dispute that a tomato grown locally is going to taste absolutely better than one shipped from across the country," and those like him, promote buying and eating area-grown produce. Eating freshly picked local produce means you get the freshest produce as well as a great benefit from the nutritional boost it gives.

Edwin went on to say, "The food that you are going to buy from local farmers is going to have so many more nutrients because it is picked ripe. It's picked when it is ready to be eaten, when the sun's energy has given it the maximum amount of flavor and sweetness."[18]

According to book author and Certified Nutritionist, Christine Avanti, in the past decade, the number of farmer's markets has exploded across the country. There are now more than 8,500 nationwide and 900 are open during the winter. That's a 250-percent increase since 1994.

---

[17] Andrea Bailey Willits, "Grow," Home Life Magazine (March 2011): 19–20. 174.
[18] Sara Askew Jones, "Healthy Living—Eat Local," Southern Living Magazine (June 2008): 109–111.

She says, "Your local farmers' market is hands-down the best place to buy fresh, locally grown food—food that's not a product of the processed food industry. I guarantee you that the fresh produce, the fresh-laid eggs, the pasture-raised beef, poultry, and pork, the jars of honey, the fresh baked bread—whatever you buy at the farmers' market—will taste better than anything you could buy at the supermarket."[19]

The benefits of buying local are: freshness, great flavor, seasonal variety, and as if that is not enough, when you buy from area farmers, more of your food dollars stay in your community. So if you do not want to grow your own—Go, go, go to your local farmers' market or vegetable urban farm and pick away!

HEALTH BENEFITS OF EATING FRESH

1. Eating raw cruciferous vegetables (such as cabbage, cauliflower, or broccoli) may help protect against the development of bladder cancer.

2. According to a new study, eating a high amount of vegetables (428 grams per day in the research) may reduce the risk of developing type 2 diabetes.

3. You avoid exposure to deadly pesticides and health risks related to their usage in planting.

4. Additives and preservatives are not being ingested into your system.

---

[19] Christine Alvanti, Skinny Chicks Eat Real Food (Emmaus, Rodale Publishing, 2012), 147–148.

CANNING TIPS

When I was a little girl, my grandparents canned the produce from their garden. It was a big part of their summer activities. What fun to pull out homemade strawberry jam, corn cut fresh from the cob, or green beans from the freezer when visiting them. Companies like Canal House help women with canning supplies, techniques, and recipes.

From an article on The Open Road Blog entitled, "Canning and Preserving, Courtesy of Canal House," the author states, "It's always a treat to receive a jar of homemade jam or preserves from a friend or neighbor at the end of berry season or during the holidays. But many home cooks—even those who are undeterred by stirring Risotto or unintimidated by flipping a Tarte Tatin—don't try canning and preserving at home. There's an unspoken assumption that pickling vegetables or jarring a batch of sauce or salsa requires a great deal of time and skill. But actually, canning and preserving are about as straightforward as they are soulful!"

She goes on to state, "Canning and preserving at home captures the essence of seasonal fruits and vegetables, making them available year round (with an extra dose of affection). Jam made with berries from a friend's garden, for instance, brings new meaning to your morning toast or a PB&J made for a child's lunch. You might try a salsa or pico de gallo recipe, especially if your tomato plants are growing like weeds in the July sunshine. Being able to open a jar of salsa at a wintertime football party, made from tomatoes that grew in your yard the previous summer, brings a soulful touch to otherwise casual snack food. Home chefs can make canning/preserving recipes their own, such as substituting blood oranges, grapefruits, tangerines, or even limes in orange marmalade recipes (although, for the record, citrus fruits are in season in the winter). While canning and preserving makes every day eating more upscale, it's not the complex, ambitious task that many people think it is. Give the Canal House Cooking canning and preserving recipes a try ... and then muster all your self-control not to open the jars before October. You'll love having these reminders of summer when you're unpacking your sweaters and holiday decorations. And you get to eat local, healthful food long after you've stopped shopping for citronella candles and sunblock." [20]

Owners of Canal House, Christopher Hirsheimer and Meredith Hamilton, were asked the following questions in an interview on Williams-Sonoma's blog titled, The Blender. "For someone who's new to preserving (canning), what would you recommend they start with? Any tips? Jam is great and easy, and you can start eating it right away—a fast return on your efforts. Make small batches of jam. You won't be overwhelmed by the whole process. Also, when you keep it small you won't overcook the fruit like when you have to boil down and reduce a large volume of liquid. When they are asked, "What will you be putting up this year? What are your favorite ingredients to preserve?" Their response is, "We always put up lots of tomatoes: tomato passata, tomato jam, oven-dried tomatoes, and on and on."

[20] "Canning and Preserving Courtesy of Canal House." http://www.openroadmedia.com/blog/2012-07-12/Can- ning-and-Preserving-Courtesy-of-Canal-House-Cooking.aspx

TOOLS FOR CANNING

- **Boiling Water Canner**—Made of porcelain-coated steel or aluminum. Comes with an airtight lid and a wire basket for holding canning jars
- **Home Canning Jars**—Found at Wal-Mart, Target, Williams-Sonoma, and local grocery stores
- **Canning Tools**—Found at Wal-Mart, Target, Williams–Sonoma, and local grocery stores. Note: For a more extensive list, see www.williams-sonoma.com (canning and preserving)

• CANNING TOMATOES[21]

1. Visually examine canning jars for nicks, cracks, uneven rims, or sharp edges that may prevent sealing or cause breakage. Examine canning lids to ensure they are free of dents and sealing compound is even and complete. Check bands for proper fit.

2. Wash jars and two-piece caps in hot, soapy water. Rinse well. Dry bands; set aside. Heat jars and lids in a saucepot of simmering water (180°F or 82°C). Do not boil lids. Allow jars and lids to remain in hot water until ready for use, removing one at a time as needed.

3. Fill boiling-water canner half-full with hot water. Elevate rack in canner. Put canner lid in place. Heat water just to a simmer (180°F or 82°C). Keep water hot until used for processing.

4. Select fresh tomatoes at their peak of quality and flavor. Use firm tomatoes free of cracks, spots, and growths. Prepare only enough for one canner load. Wash tomatoes; drain.

5. Place tomatoes in wire basket and lower into a large saucepot of boiling water. Blanch tomatoes 30 to 60 seconds or until skins start to crack. Remove from boiling water. Dip immediately into cold water.

6. Slip off skins; trim away any green areas; cut out core. Leave tomatoes whole or cut into halves or quarters. For tomatoes packed in water, place tomatoes in a large saucepot, adding just enough water to cover. Boil gently 5 minutes. Remove canning jar from hot water with a jar lifter; set jar on towel. Add 1 tablespoon bottled lemon juice to each pint jar or 2 tablespoons bottled lemon juice to each quart jar.

7. Carefully pack tomatoes into hot jar, leaving ½-inch headspace. Ladle boiling water or cooking liquid over tomatoes, leaving ½-inch headspace. Add ½ teaspoon salt per pint jar or 1 teaspoon salt per quart jar, if desired.

8. Slide a non-metallic spatula between tomatoes and jar; press back gently on tomatoes to release trapped air bubbles. Repeat procedure 2 to 3 times around inside of jar.

9. Wipe rim and threads of jar with a clean, damp cloth. Remove lid from hot water using a lid wand. Place lid on jar, centering sealing compound on rim. Screw band down evenly and firmly, just until resistance is met—fingertip tight.

[21] Roger Doiron, "Canning Tomatoes Step by Step," Kitchen Gardener's International. http://kgi.org/canning-tomatoes-step-step

10. As each jar is filled, set it onto the elevated rack in the boiling-water canner. Water in canner should be kept at a simmer (180°F or 82°C). After all jars are filled and placed onto the rack, lower rack into canner. Water must cover the two-piece caps on the jars by 1 to 2 inches. Add boiling water, if necessary. Put lid on canner. Bring water to a boil. Start counting processing time after water comes to a rolling boil. Process pints 40 minutes, quarts 45 minutes, at a gentle but steady boil for altitudes at or below 1,000 feet above sea level. For higher altitude areas, consult your local extension office.

11. When processing time is complete, turn off heat and remove canner lid. Let canner cool minutes before removing jars. Remove jars from canner and set them upright, 1 to 2 inches apart, on a dry towel to cool. Do not retighten bands. Let jars cool 12 to 24 hours.

12. After jars have cooled, check lids for a seal by pressing on the center of each lid. If the center is pulled down and does not flex, remove the band, and gently try to lift the lid off with your fingertips. If the lid does not flex and you cannot lift it off, the lid has a good vacuum seal.

13. Wipe lid and jar surface with a clean, damp cloth to remove food particles or residue. Label. Store jars in a cool, dry, dark place.

CANNING RECIPES

Peach Preserves

3 teaspoons Fruit Fresh®

¼ cup water

1 cup sugar

1 quart sliced and peeled peaches

Mix Fruit Fresh® and water with sliced peaches. Pour sugar over fruit but do not stir. Let soak covered in refrigerator for 12 hours. The sugar will make a juice without adding more water. Cook on stovetop in a thick pot for 2 to 3 hours until juice becomes thickened and takes on the look of preserves. Fruit will be soft. Do not cook more than 6 quarts at a time. Each recipe makes a quart of peach preserves. Once completely cooked, place in quart size jars. Seal top with paraffin wax. Be careful when you melt the paraffin not to leave it atop stove after melted; wax can be flammable. Use 2 to 3 teaspoons of melted paraffin to top each jar of preserves. Secure with jar lid.

Olita's Sweet Pickles

1 gallon jar of whole dill pickles

5 pounds sugar

8 to 10 ounces minced garlic

10 to 12 cinnamon sticks

Drain juice from pickles and rinse. Slice pickles. Return to jar and layer pickles, sugar, garlic, and cinnamon sticks. Replace jar lid and tape around edges. Turn upside down daily for 14 days. Keep refrigerated after opening.

Bread and Butter Pickles

5½ cups pickling cucumbers, thinly sliced

1½ tablespoons kosher salt

1 cup sweet onion, thinly sliced

1 cup granulated white sugar

1 cup white vinegar

½ cup apple cider vinegar

¼ cup light brown sugar (packed)

1½ teaspoons mustard seeds

⅛ teaspoon ground turmeric

Combine cucumbers and salt in a large, shallow bowl; cover and chill 1½ hours. Move cucumbers into a colander and rinse thoroughly under cold water. Drain well, and return cucumbers to bowl. Add onion to the bowl. Combine sugar and remaining ingredients in a medium saucepan; bring to a simmer over medium heat, stirring until sugar dissolves. Pour hot vinegar mixture over cucumber mixture; let stand at room temperature 1 hour. Cover and refrigerate 24 hours. Store in an airtight container in refrigerator up to 2 weeks. Yields 4 cups of pickles.

Spaghetti Sauce

- 25 pounds tomatoes (about 80 medium)
- 4 large green peppers, seeded
- 4 large onions, cut into wedges
- 2 cans (12 ounces each) tomato paste
- ¼ cup canola oil
- 2/3 cup sugar
- ¼ cup salt
- 8 garlic cloves, minced
- 4 teaspoons dried oregano
- 2 teaspoons dried parsley flakes
- 2 teaspoons dried basil
- 2 teaspoons crushed red pepper flakes
- 2 teaspoons Worcestershire sauce
- 2 bay leaves
- 1 cup plus 2 tablespoons bottled lemon juice

In a Dutch oven, bring 2 quarts water to a boil. Using a slotted spoon, place tomatoes, one at a time, in boiling water for 30-60 seconds. Remove each tomato and immediately plunge into ice water. Peel and quarter tomatoes; place in a stockpot. Pulse green peppers and onions in batches in a food processor until finely chopped; transfer to stockpot. Stir in next 11 ingredients. Add water to cover; bring to a boil. Reduce heat; simmer, uncovered, 4-5 hours, stirring occasionally. Discard bay leaves. Add 2 tablespoons lemon juice to each of nine hot 1-qt. jars. Ladle hot mixture into jars, leaving ½-inch headspace. Remove air bubbles and adjust headspace, if necessary, by adding or removing hot mixture. Wipe rims. Center lids on jars; screw on bands until fingertip tight. Place jars into canner with simmering water, ensuring that they are completely covered with water. Bring to a boil; process for 40 minutes. Remove jars and cool.

Heirloom Tomato Salsa

- 5 pounds heirloom tomatoes
- 2 onions, roughly chopped
- 4 large cloves of garlic, roughly chopped
- 1 cup fresh cilantro leaves, washed, and dried
- 1 tablespoon sea salt
- 1 to 2 jalapeño peppers, seeds, ribs, and stems removed, finely diced (wear gloves when working with these)
- ¼ cup sugar
- 1½ cups white vinegar

Place the tomatoes, onions, garlic, and cilantro in the bowl of a food processor and blend until it reaches the desired consistency. Put the blended mixture into a large, non-reactive pot, add the jalapeños, sugar, salt, and vinegar, bring to a boil, and then simmer until it reaches the desired thickness. While the salsa is cooking, sterilize your jars and lids in the hot water bath for 10 minutes. Drain and remove the jars, ladle the hot salsa directly into the hot jars leaving ¼ head space, wipe the rims with a clean, damp paper towel, apply the lids, and secure the bands. Process in a hot water bath canner for 20 minutes, then remove from the water and let the jars cool on a rack or several dishtowels to avoid extreme temperature changes, which can crack the jars. Once cooled, check the seals (the lids must be popped down) and store in a cool dark place for up to one year. If any of the lids have not sealed properly, store the jar in the fridge and use within one week. Yields: 6 pints or 12 half-pints.

Chow Chow

12½ pounds green tomatoes, chopped

8 large onions, chopped,

10 green bell peppers, chopped

3 teaspoons salt

6 chopped green Chile peppers

1 quart distilled white vinegar

½ cup prepared horseradish

1 tablespoon ground cinnamon

1 tablespoon ground allspice

¼ teaspoon ground cloves

Combine tomatoes, onions, bell peppers, and salt in a large bowl. Let stand overnight. Drain the mixture and add hot Chile peppers, vinegar, sugar, and horseradish. Wrap the cinnamon, allspice, and cloves in a cheesecloth or porous bag, and add to the mixture. Boil the mixture for 15 minutes, or until tender. Pack tightly in sterilized jars and seal. Store the jars in a cool, dark place for at least two weeks to allow the flavors to mingle. Store unopened for up to a year. Refrigerate after opening.

Barbecue Sauce

6 tablespoons brown sugar

3 tablespoons paprika

3 teaspoons salt

3 teaspoons dry mustard

1 teaspoon chili powder

⅛ teaspoon cayenne pepper

6 tablespoons Worcestershire sauce

3 cups tomato juice

¾ cup chili sauce

¾ cup vinegar

1 ½ cups onions, finely chopped

In saucepan, mix all ingredients and boil for 15 minutes over medium-high heat, stirring occasionally. Pour into sterilized canning jars to within a ½ inch of the top. Place cap on and screw tightly to seal. Place in a boiling *water bath* for 10 minutes. A *water bath* is a method of processing fruits, tomatoes, and pickles. For *water bath*: Use a large kettle or pail that is deep enough to cover jars at least one inch over the top and a little extra space for boiling. A wire rack is necessary for the bottom of the kettle or pail in order for the jars to be held at least one inch above the bottom of the pan. This will allow water to circulate. Cover the pan to keep water at a rolling boil during the process. As soon as water reaches a good boil, begin your *water bath* time of 10 minutes. Make sure the water is boiling during the processing period. When time is up, remove jars and allow to cool completely. Check lids to make sure they are tight and secure. Store in a cool place.

TIPS FOR GARDENING, FLOWER BEDS, AND POTTED PLANTS

African Violet—Pour the water from boiled eggs on your African violets. They will thrive on the extra calcium.

Ants—If you place black pepper in the haunts of ants, they will flee! Also, did you know that ants will not cross a chalk-drawn line?

Arrangements of fresh tulips stay fresher when copper pennies are tossed into the water.

A teaspoon of sugar to soapy lather will remove gardening stains from your hands.

Azaleas—One tablespoon of vinegar to one gallon of water when you are watering azaleas and other acid-loving plants such as hydrangeas and gardenias will correct any yellowing of the plants.

Azaleas—Azaleas thrive when you spray them every three weeks with a solution of water and ammonia. Use 1 level teaspoon ammonia to one gallon of water for the spray.

Blackberries make a great addition to the garden. They can be grown easily along a fence or wall. Space plants 4 to 5 feet apart. Johnson's Nursery or Petals from the Past are good sources for purchasing blackberry plants. Place order at www.johnsonnursery.com or www.petalsfromthepast.com. [22]

Black Spot and Mildew—Garlic bulbs planted near rose bushes will help the bushes develop resistance to black spot and mildew.

Blueberries in a Container—Purchase a rabbit eye blueberry (favorites are "Delite" and "Tifblue") from your local nursery. Plant it in a large container filled with good soil and peat moss; then water thoroughly. Place it in partial to full sun and mulch well to help the plant retain moisture. Containers dry out quickly in heat of summer, so check daily. Use an azalea fertilizer in the spring and fall. This plant will look great and add color to your porch year round, as well as provide blueberries for you to enjoy for a month or so in the summer. [23]

Box Planter—Begin with a small, hardy shrub such as a dwarf Alberta spruce, as a permanent anchor. Renew the spaces around the spruce with a variety of fresh seasonal annuals. Use small annuals that won't overwhelm the shrub and slow-release fertilizer when you plant. [24]

Day Lilies—There are over 50,000 named daylily selections. Some of the favorites are Tuscawilla, Red Volunteer, Orange Volunteer, Vanilla Fluff, and Strawberry Candy.

Drain Spouts—To save topsoil and prevent erosion of lawn and garden from drain spouts, place a large flat stone under the spout to spread the rain water over a larger area.

Dwarf pineapple lilies add a lush appearance to the front of a border. These beautiful plants originated in South Africa. They got their name from the pineapple-shaped tufts of green leaflike bracts that form atop their flower spikes. Choose from several varieties. Add an unusual texture and look by trying pineapple lilies in your flowerbeds.

---

[22] Rebecca bull Reed, "Home and Garden- Family of Flowers," *Southern Living* (May 2008): 50–54.
[23] "A Harvest by the Door," *Southern Living* (May 2008): 18.
[24] Kate Carter Fredrick, "Outdoor Containers—Four Seasons," *Better Homes and Gardens* (March 2010): 130–134.

Food—A good slow-release fertilizer will feed plants for up to three months.

French Hydrangeas—These beautiful southern plants have voluptuous blossoms. They prefer morning sun with light afternoon shade. Soil pH can affect the color of the blossoms. Acid soil produces the bluest blues; white alkaline soil can turn blossoms pink. Hydrangeas make a great cut flower for indoor arrangements. Cuttings: Take 6 to 8-inch cuttings, wet the end, dip in rooting powder, and then stick each cutting into moist potting soil. Keep soil moist and plant in shade. Cutting should root in six to eight weeks. Place in garden bed. Hint: For pink blooms sprinkle, one tablespoon lime around the base. For blue, sprinkle 1 tablespoon aluminum sulfate at the base.[25]

Frost Dates—To learn when the last frost date in your area should occur before planting spring plants, visit www.victoryseeds.com/frost

Gardenias—A sprinkling of Epsom salt around the roots will reward you with longer blooms.

Great Tool—Water your garden with a Rain Wand. Its aluminum extension and nozzle let you apply a shower of water to your plants and control the amount with an easy-grip shut-off handle. Can be purchased at any nursery or garden store.

Great Vines—Vines offer great solutions for color, fragrance, and shade in tight spots. Good choices include Tangerine Beauty cross vine with orange-red flowers; Carolina Jessamine with fragrant, yellow blooms; and trumpet honeysuckle with red and yellow flowers.[26]

Hanging Baskets—Water your hanging plants with ice cubes to eliminate any dripping.

Healthier Geraniums—Coffee grounds added to soil when you are planting geraniums increase growth and blossoms.

House Plants—Before you leave town on a trip, place your houseplants on bricks in the bathtub filled with water. Enough water will be absorbed into the bricks to keep the plants in good condition (only for pots with drainage).

Making a Flower Bed—Composted cow manure or mushroom compost adds nutrients; pulverized bark or soil conditioner improves texture; and topsoil adds volume for building up the bed.

Marigolds—Signet Marigold is an excellent flowering plant for window boxes, herb gardens, and in front of mixed borders. Hundreds of tiny flowers will appear all summer amid scented foliage. Planting only a half-inch deep, these plants will yield flowers into the fall.[27]

Moles—If you have problems with moles in the yard, place coffee grounds in their runs.

Mosquitoes—You can reduce the number of mosquitoes breeding in your yard by emptying all sources of water from buckets and plant saucers. Keep roof gutters clear of debris so water does not collect. Fill low spots in yard and flowerbeds where water tends to stand. Mosquito Bits (granules) or Mosquito Dunks (solid) are good products for ridding your yard of these pesky critters. A sprig of fresh mint rubbed on face, arms, and legs repels mosquitoes.[28]

---

[25] Gene B. Bussell, "Home and Garden Plants We Love—Summertime Blues," *Southern Living* (June 2008).
[26] "Home and Garden—Things to Do," *Southern Living* (March 2008): 62.
[27] Steve Bender, "Home and Garden Plants We Love—Try This Marigold," *Southern Living* (May 2008): 85–87.
[28] "Flowers You'll Love: Around the Garden," *Southern Living* (August 2007): 55–56

Pansies—These flowers may be the most versatile garden annual. They have a vast array of colors, thrive in chilly weather, and do equally well in beds and containers. In the spring, you can plant well before the frost and in the fall, you can plant them in September while the days are still warm. You will enjoy their color right into November, if not longer. [29]

Perennial Color—Purple Cone flower is a great choice for your garden and you will enjoy it year after year. Varieties include the Ruby Star, Bravado, White Swan, and White Luster. All prefer well-drained soil. Improve drainage by adding some organic matter, such composted manure, finely shredded pine bark or mushroom compost. After planting water them well until established. [30]

Pick tomatoes, peppers, and tomatillos early in the morning the day you plan to eat them. Use sharp clippers to harvest these to avoid tearing the vines.

Pruning—When pruning azaleas, forsythias, spiraeas, and quince, they should be trimmed once they have finished blooming. If you wait until summer to cut them back, you will remove next year's flowers.

Quick Spring Arrangement—Daffodils look great when placed as a bunch in a small vase. When cutting the daffodils, cut the stems at an angle under water to improve water uptake. These flowers secrete a substance that prevents other flowers from taking in water, so mix them only with other daffodils. Place the arrangement in a cool area away from vents and direct sunlight; be sure to change the water every couple of days. For freshness, add oral preservative. [31]

Rabbits and Squirrels—Moth balls sprinkled by tomato plants and other fruits will keep squirrels and rabbits away. [32]

Roses—As the days become warmer and leaves begin to appear on your roses, fertilize with Schultz Liquid Rose food 10-12-12 or a granular feed such as Vigoro Rose Plant Food 12-6-10. Amend the soil around your rose bushes by adding mushroom compost or composted manure is great for rose bushes.

Unwanted Grass—For unwanted grass on your patio or walkway, pour table salt between the stones and/or bricks.

Weeds—To stop weeds and grass from running wild between your patio bricks, douse them with a little ammonia and they will promptly die.

White Vinegar—Fill a spray bottle with vinegar and spray to kill weeds in garden, yard, and pots. Flowering plants should be trimmed once they are finished blooming. If you wait until summer, you will hinder the plant from producing foliage in the coming year.

Wilted Cut Flowers—A teaspoon of household dish detergent to one quart of water will revive wilted cut flowers. [33]

---

[29] Eric Liskey, "Outdoors Plantings—Pansy Power," Better Homes and Gardens (March 2010): 112–114.
[30] Rebecca bull Reed, "Home and Garden—Family of Flowers," Southern Living (May 2008): 50–54.
[31] "Home and Garden—Things to Do," Southern Living (March 2008): 62.
[32] Wimmer Cookbooks, Why Didn't I Think of That? (Memphis, Wimmerco.com 1993), 80.
[33] Melanie Gaines, "Summer Pleasures: Colorful Cuttings," Decorating Step-by-Step (May 2007): 128.

Barbara Mundall of *Better Homes and Garden Magazine* says, "One of the most difficult challenges gardeners face is getting the garden to look good for more than one moment in time. Her solution, a valuable lesson for all gardeners, is to cultivate a diversity of plants, including species that bloom later and sport attractive, long-lasting foliage. As the earliest plants finish blooming or die back, ferns unfurl and hostas begin to poke their shoots through the soil. Then rhododendrons, peonies, and hydrangeas add season-long succession of blooms, ensuring that when spring finally arrives, it will be in no hurry to leave."[34]

RESOURCE BOOKS

A Field Guide to Trees and Shrubs by George A. Petrides

Ball Blue Book—The Guide to Home Canning and Container Gardening for All Seasons by Barbara Wise

Encyclopedia of Garden Plants by Christopher Brickell

Herbs and Spices: The Cook's Reference by Jill Norman

Herb Gardening from the Ground Up by Sal Gilbertie

Landscape for Privacy: Innovative Ways to Turn Your Outdoor Space Into a Peaceful Retreat by Marty Wingate

Organic Gardening: A Practical Guide to Natural Gardens by Michael and Christine Lavelle

Raised-Up Vegetable Gardening Made Simple by Raymond Nones

Real Food: For Mother and Baby by Nina Planck

Real Food: What to Eat and Why by Nina Planck

Residential Landscape Design for the Horticulturally Hopeless by Mike Dooley

The American Horticultural Society—A-Z by Christopher Brickell

The Backyard Homestead by Carleen Madigan

The Cook's Herb Garden by Jeff Cox and Marie Pierre Moine

The Farmers Market Cookbook by Nina Planck

The Vegetable Gardner's Bible by Edward C. Smith

The Vegetable Gardener's Container Bible by Edward C. Smith

Timeless Landscape Design—The Four-Part Master Plan by Hugh Dagner and Mary Palmer Dagner

---

[34] Barbara Mundall, "Outdoors in the Garden—Spring Times," Better Homes and Garden, (March 2010): 95–99.

LYDIA
An Hospitable Woman

Biblical Principle: Women changed by the truth of the gospel will exercise their spiritual gifting for the glory of God.

Read Acts 16:13-15 (9-12).

1. What was the vision Paul had that led him to Philippi in the district of Macedonia?

2. On which day of the week did Paul and his disciples meet a group of women on the riverbank outside of Philippi? What were they doing?

3. What woman was described as "a merchant of expensive purple cloth? What else did Luke say about her?

4. What happened to Lydia as she listened to Paul preach the gospel?

5. The truth of the gospel penetrates the heart and changes lives. Have you come to the place Lydia came to of allowing the gospel to penetrate your heart and change your life? Explain.

6. Lydia was an hospitable woman. What did she offer to do for Paul and his disciples?

7. What spiritual gift was Lydia demonstrating? What was it in Lydia's life that changed her heart and made her willing to minister to Paul, Luke, and Silas?

8. What admonishment is given believers in Romans 12:13?

9. What did you learn from Lydia's story?

Week Eight Notes

What I Learned Today

Week Nine

WOMAN TO WOMAN

Introduction
WISE COUNSEL

*Y*ears ago, when God chose to begin writing my and Mark's life story quite differently from what I had imagined it would be, I was struggling emotionally and spiritually. I needed to talk to a woman who was older, wiser, and one that I admired and who could be trusted with my feelings. So, I sought the counsel of an older woman in our church. At the time, she directed the prayer ministry and had a private office; so we met there on a Sunday afternoon.

Carolyn, fondly known as Miss Higgy (for Higginbotham), was always smiling and addressed everyone she saw as, "Sweetie." That day, I rounded the corner to her office to be greeted with a big smile and, "Well, Sweetie, come on in. Sit down. Before you share with me what is on your heart, let me pray for us." She prayed, and as I began to share with her, a dam broke wide open and tears were flowing like water out of a broken pipe! I poured my heart out to her. I felt bad for Miss Higgy as I desperately tried to explain my struggle through tears, sniffles, and an unsteady voice. She sat there patiently listening and handing me Kleenex after Kleenex. I was amazed that she could understand a word I said, but she seemed to comprehend my struggle.

When I had finished talking and dried my tears, she said to me, "Sweetie, I want you to stay away from the 'What if's' and the 'If only's.' Those are Satan's playground. He will cause you to struggle with doubt and fear, and he will have you questioning God, instead of trusting Him." I'm not sure how she knew that in months past, I had said to Mark many times, "If only we had…" or "What if we had done this instead of that, things would be different." Despite my tears and unsteady voice, the Spirit allowed her to know the word I needed to hear that day. She was so right! I had allowed Satan a foothold through questioning God and His plan for our lives.

---

*S*ince that day, I have thought about Miss Higgy's words of advice to me many times and I have used them time after time when counseling young women. Miss Higgy loved me, challenged me, and encouraged me. In the Bible we see older women loving and encouraging young women. Naomi loved and encouraged Ruth; Elizabeth loved and encouraged Mary.

God knew that young women would need the love, counsel, and encouragement of older women, which is why he placed a mandate or a challenge in the Bible for older women to teach and admonish young women. How grateful I am for Miss Higgy and other older women who have invested in my life through the way they lived, loved, and served.

It is a wise young woman who seeks time with and counsel and instruction from an older woman. Nothing in your life can hold as much value as the influence of an older woman who has experienced a long walk with Christ, many years of marriage, and a faithful trust in God, who has chosen to write her life story to be told!

My sweet mentor and dear friend, Carolyn Higginbotham, affectionately known as "Miss Higgy," passed away on January 22, 2017. I will be forever grateful for her profound impact upon my life.

LIVING AND LOVING *with Purpose*

Years ago, I read this statement in a book, "When we trust our lives to the unseen but ever-present God, he will write our lives into His story, and every last one of them will turn out to be a great read." Whether you are a college, single, or young married woman, God is writing your story and it will be a great read!

If you have ever read an autobiography, you have read the life story of the person featured in the book, written by that person. As children of God, He writes our story, and every one of us can be sure "it will be a good read." You can trust Him to write your story, direct your steps, and accomplish what He desires, according to His will and His timing.

God writes our stories to be told. We can learn from one another's stories. Let's look at some of the stories God has written in the lives of simple, gentle, quiet women used of God to impact thousands—women who lived, loved, and served others with great purpose. Perhaps their stories will have a profound impact on your life.

Amy Carmichael was a young woman who, at a very young age, felt called by God to the mission field. She followed God's guidance and eventually went to India to serve. There, she ministered to the people of that country for fifty-three years without a furlough. She founded an orphanage called the Dohnavur Foundation. It was a refuge for children in moral danger—unwanted children who were orphaned. She became the mother to hundreds of thousands of children. Amy was fondly known as Amma. She was a young woman who sacrificed all for the love of her Savior and His call on her life. Elisabeth Elliott said of Amy, "So she finished her course—Amy Carmichael, one of the tens of thousands of lovers of the Lord who staked everything on His faithfulness. Her life is another case in point of how grace goes to work on the raw material of individual nature. Was she a fool? Yes, for the same reason the apostle Paul was: for Christ's sake."[35] Amy allowed God to write her story and because she did, her life of obedience and courage is a model for all Christian women.

Sherry Blankenship is a pastor's wife in St. Louis, Missouri. I first read her story in a book titled *Draw Near*. Her story is one that I am certain, if God had given her a choice, she would have chosen not to have it written the way He chose to write it. Sherry gave birth to triplets in September of 1981, two boys, Joshua and Jonathan, and a little girl named Anna Joy. This caught my attention as I began to read because our youngest daughter was born in September of 1981. Anna Joy was a wonderful little girl who was very fond of her two brothers. At the age of thirteen, she began to run a low-grade fever and was unusually tired. Having been a track runner, an A student, and full of life, this change in her behavior alarmed her mother. Sherry, being concerned, ordered blood work at their doctor's office. The doctor called following the first draw of blood and asked for a second set of blood to be drawn and tested. When the results came in, Anna was diagnosed with leukemia. Shocked and disheartened, they took Anna to St. Louis Children's Hospital. Her book is a record of her daily journal and journey with Anna over a year and a half of treatments, mountaintops, valleys, pain, and heartache. Yet in the midst of it all, God was there. Anna's life and radiance drew others to her heavenly Father as she lived out

[35] Elisabeth Elliot, *A Chance to Die*. (Revell Publishing, 1987).

the story written for her. This young woman was called to suffer and ultimately die; her mother, Sherry, along with her dad and brothers, called to walk that hard road with her. But oh the testimony of God's faithfulness and grace that is found in the midst of this story. God wrote their story so that others can see and know the love of a mother for her child and the love and faithfulness of our heavenly Father.[36]

Mary was a young woman, sweet, innocent, full of life, and deeply in love with her heavenly Father and a young man named Joseph. She was filled with excitement and joy at the thought of their wedding to come. Oh, the planning that lay ahead of her. Her story was an exciting one, a story every young woman dreams of—a handsome young man, devoted to her and his heavenly Father. Their future looked so bright. Then God informed Mary of a new chapter he had written for her life. One she was unaware of prior to a visit from an angel named Gabriel. He informed Mary that God was about to rewrite her future; she had been chosen by God to bear His son. The angel said to her, "Rejoice, highly favored one, the Lord is with you; blessed are you among women." Mary's response was one that is an example to all women, when God writes our stories differently than we imagined. "I am the Lord's servant. May everything you have said about me come true." Because of Mary's willingness to submit to God's divine plan, she was given the honor of being the mother of the Savior of the world. She was a blessed woman, because she was an obedient woman.

Mary's story—God's story!

All three of these women are uniquely different from one another, living in various times in history. Mary's story was written nearly two thousand years ago and Amy's was written in the 1800's. Sherry's and Anna Joy's stories were written in this day and time. Each woman is an example of a woman willing to submit her life to the Master author, as He writes her story with His pen and for His purposes.

No matter where you are in life, if you are willing to submit to God, he will write a story that will be a "good read"—a story with a grand ending!

*For since the world began, no ear has heard and no eye has seen
a God like you, who works for those who wait for Him.
Isaiah 64:4 NLV*

*Trust in the Lord with all your heart, and lean not on your own understanding;
in all your ways acknowledge Him, and He shall direct your paths.
Proverbs 3:5 NKJV*

---

[36] Sherry Blankenship, *Draw Near.* (Tate Publishing, 2007). 199.

SINGLE AND LIVING *Intentionally*

by Leslie Hollowell

I came to an understanding years ago that "Many are the plans in a person's heart, but it's the Lord's purpose that prevails." Proverbs 19:21 NIV

I began at the early age of eight striving to determine the plans for my life. At this point, I was determined to be a detective and take my place as the fourth angel on Charlie's Angels. By age twelve, I was going to be a news anchorwoman. I sat for hours in the bathroom with my round brush, practicing my "and now for our local weather" voice.

Next up were my high school years. It was in that season of life that I realized I had a flair for teaching. My former third-grade teacher permitted me to "teach" a few lessons every week for a short period of time when I was her teacher's aide. It was then that I found my calling. I proceeded down the road of elementary education and started striving to set my life plans in order.

At eighteen years of age, I began college. I was determined to get my degree, a job, followed by marriage, then have children and enjoy summers off for family vacations. Well, I did end up with a fun job teaching first grade. I truly loved it, but I was still missing several parts of my plan—husband, children, and family vacations!

Fortunately, while in college, I had the privilege of being discipled! Through that experience, I realized that single or married, God had called me to be intentional in investing my life in others. I began striving to do that whenever God opened a door. I went on many youth trips as a counselor, spent summers working for BREAKAWAY Ministries, mentored girls at the Big Oak Girls Ranch, and found complete joy in living out 2 Timothy 2:2. I absolutely loved being able to teach and disciple others what God had so graciously taught me through those who had discipled me.

But, I was still lonely for my life mate. I remember praying and crying many nights and telling God, despite the loneliness, "I choose You!" I watched friend after friend get married and have children. Some days the loneliness seemed unbearable. And yet, it pushed me to the feet of Jesus and made me cling to His Word for hope and security. I learned I had to be intentional in my walk with the Lord, and so I sought to strive to do whatever I could not to fall prey to the ways of the world.

As time went on, God truly proved His faithfulness in my life. I laugh at the fact that I can quote nearly all the verses in the Bible on "waiting." I will tell you now that without a doubt, God's timing is Worth the Wait! I met the most amazing man at thirty-six years of age and married him one month before my thirty-eighth birthday. Now, in my forties, I am a mother to the cutest, most adorable little boy ever, and I can confidently say that God's timing is perfect! He is trustworthy, faithful, and He knows the plans He has for you!

INTENTIONAL LIVING AS WIFE AND MOM
by Angela Porada

I want to be INTENTIONAL about my role as a wife and mom. Intentional is defined as "done with intention or purpose; pointing beyond self." Therefore, I want our home to be a SAFE place, a place where my husband and children are filled up to go out and face the world. I want to take the word SAFE and use each letter to express the ways in which I desire to be intentional in my home.

S-SPIRITUALLY SAFE

- A home where everyone is free to ask questions
- A home where there is always time for conversation
- A home of unselfishness, not about me or my time

A-ACCEPTED

- A home where everyone is accepted regardless of his/her behavior; the person is accepted not the bad behavior
- A home where making fun of one another is not tolerated
- A home where differences are appreciated and accepted

F-FUN

- A home filled with laughter, music, games, and lots of noise
- A home where outdoor play is continual
- A home where spending time together is valued
- A home where cleaning is set aside, if need be, in order to have time as a family

E-ENGAGED/EDUCATIONAL

- A home where each family member is engaged in the lives of one another
- A home where dates as a couple are a priority
- A home where individual time is scheduled with each child
- A home where going to sporting events and outside activities to support one another is expected
- A home where teaching the children God's Word is first and foremost
- A home where education is valued and self-discipline and individual effort is expected whether in homeschooling (if God has called you to this), or attending public or private school

SEVERAL WAYS GOD HAS SHOWN ME
How to be Intentional

1. Obedience to God's Word—I have to rise early and spend time in the Word

2. I am to take every thought captive to the obedience of Christ

3. Submit to whatever it is God is asking me to do

4. Pray it; don't say it!

5. Turn off the television

6. Let the little things go

7. Allow the Lord to show me how I can meet the needs of my husband and family

8. Don't criticize my husband to my friends or my family

9. Praying and preparing before approaching my husband about sensitive or difficult subjects, and doing it with a calm, loving, and gentle spirit

Intentional Living Will Make My Home, and Your Home, a Safe Place for All Who Live There!

READING RESOURCES

WOMEN'S BOOKS:

A Lifetime of Wisdom by Joni Erickson Tada

A Loving Life by Paul E. Miller

A Place of Healing: Wrestling with the Mystery of Suffering by Joni Erickson Tada

A Praying Life by Paul E. Miller

A Young Woman After God's Own Heart by Elizabeth George

A Young Woman's Guide to Making Right Decisions by Elizabeth George

A Young Woman's Walk with God: Growing More Like Jesus by Elizabeth George

Before You Meet Prince Charming: A Guide to Radiant Beauty by Sarah Mally

Calm My Anxious Heart by Linda Dillow

Chance to Die—The Life and Legacy of Amy Carmichael by Elizabeth Elliott

Courtesy and Kindness for Young Ladies by Emilie Barnes

Even Better Than Eden: Nine Ways the Bible's Story Changes Everything About Your Story by Nancy Guthrie

Every Young Woman's Battle: Guarding Your Mind by Shannon Ethridge and Stephen Arterburn

Gladys Aylward: The Adventure of a Lifetime by Janet and Geoff Benge

Green Leaf in Drought by Isobel Kuhn

Growing in Gratitude: Rediscovering the Joy of a Thankful Heart by Mary Mohler

Growing Your Faith by Jerry Bridges

His Princess—Love Letters from the King by Sheri Rose Shepherd

Kisses from Katie by Katie Davis Major

Lady in Waiting—Becoming God's Best While Waiting for Mr. Right by Jackie Kendall and Debby Jones

Lessons from the Upper Room by Sinclair Ferguson

Let Me Be a Woman by Elizabeth Elliott

Lies Young Women Believe by Nancy DeMoss Wolgemuth

Making a Difference: Impacting Culture and Society as a Christian by R.C. Sproul

Mothers and Daughters: Growing Into Wise Women Together by Nancy Wilson (Audio Book on CD)

Pathway to Freedom by Alistair Begg

Persistent Prayer by Guy Richard

Praying for Your Future Husband: Preparing Your Heart for His by Robin Jones Gunn

Right Now Counts Forever by R.C. Sproul

Sanctification: Transformed Life by David Campbell

Strength for the Weary by Derek Thomas

The Beauty of Divine Grace by Gabe Fluhrer

The Discipline of Grace by Jerry Bridges

The Hiding Place by Corrie ten Boom

The Hunger for Significance by R.C. Sproul

The Indwelling Life of Christ by Major W. Ian Thomas

The Jesus You Can't Ignore by John MacArthur

The Red Sea Rules by Robert J. Morgan

The Wise Woman and Other Stories by George MacDoanld

Transformed: Life-Taker to Life-Giver by Karen Hodge and Susan Hunt

Twelve Extraordinary Women by John MacArthur

MARRIAGE BOOKS:

A Lifelong Love by Gary L. Thomas

As Long as We Both Shall Live by Gary Smalley and Ted Cunningham

A Look at Life From a Deer Stand by Steve Chapman

Boundaries in Marriage by Dr. Henry Cloud and Dr. John Townsend

Cherish by Gary L. Thomas

Created to Be His Help Meet by Debi Pearl

Devotions for a Sacred Marriage by Gary L. Thomas

Disciplines of a Godly Man by R. Kent Hughes

Every Man's Marriage by Stephen Arterburn

Have a New Husband by Friday by Dr. Kevin Leman

Hidden Keys of a Loving and Lasting Marriage by Gary Smalley

His Needs—Her Needs by Willard F. Harley, Jr.

How We Can Build a Godly Marriage by Mary Becke and Joel Becke

Intended for Pleasure by Ed Wheat, M.D.

Intimacy Ignited by Joseph Dillow

Intimate Issues by Linda Dillow

Lasting Love: How to Avoid Marital Failure by Alistair Begg

Love and Respect for a Lifetime by Dr. Emerson Eggerichs

Love and War by John Eldredge

Masculine Mandate: God's Calling to Men by Richard Phillips

Night Light: A Devotional for Couples by Dr. James Dobson and Shirley Dobson

Passages of Marriage by Mary Alice Minirth

Pray Big for Your Marriage by Will Davis

Quiet Times for Couples by H. Norm Wright

Romantic Lovers: The Intimate Marriage by David Hocking

Sacred Marriage by Gary L. Thomas

Sheet Music by Dr. Kevin Leman

The Excellent Wife by Martha Peace

The Five Love Languages by Gary Chapman

The Four Seasons of Marriage: Secrets to a Lasting Marriage by Gary Chapman

The Power of a Praying Wife by Stormie Omartian

The Power of a Praying Husband by Stormie Omartian

What's It Like to Be Married to Me? by Linda Dillow

Young and In Love by Ted Cunningham

IN-LAW RELATIONSHIPS:

Grandmas and Mother-in-Laws: Onto the Next Thing by Nancy Wilson (Audio Book-CD)

In-Laws: Married with Parents by Wayne Mack

In-Law Relationship: The Chapman Guide to Becoming Friends with Your In-Laws by Gary Chapman

Peacemaking for Families by Ken Sande

The Message of Ruth by David J. Atkinson

The Mother-in-Law Dance: Can Two Women Love the Same Man and Still Get Along? by Annie Chapman

What's a Mother-in-Law to Do?: Essentials to Building a Loving Relationship with Your Son's New Wife by Jane Angelich

PARENTING/FAMILY:

Bible History ABC'S: God's Story from A to Z by Stephen Nichols

Boundaries with Kids by John Townsend

Brave Dad: Raising Your Kids to Love and Follow God by John F. MacArthur

Bringing Up Boys by James Dobson

Bringing Up Girls by James Dobson

Cheers to the Diaper Years by Erin Brown Hollis

Do Not Hinder Them by Justin Peters

Faith of a Child by Art Murphy

Gospel-Powered Parenting: How the Gospel Shapes and Transforms Parenting by William P. Farley

Grace Based Parenting by Tim Kimmel

Have a New Kid by Friday by Kevin Leman

It Starts at Home by Kurt Bruner and Steve Stropp

Little Steps, Big Faith by Dawn Rundman

Motherhood: Idols of a Mother's Heart by Christina Fox

Parenting with Loving Correction by Sam Crabtree

Shepherding a Child's Heart by Tedd Tripp

Siblings without Rivalry by Adele Faber

The Big Book of Questions and Answers About Jesus by Sinclair Ferguson

The Duties of Parents: Parenting God's Way by J.C. Ryle

The Family You Always Wanted to Be—5 Ways You Can Make It Happen by Gary L. Chapman

The 5 Love Languages of Children by Gary Chapman and Ross Campbell

The Magnificent Time Machine by Sinclair Ferguson

The New Birth Order Book by Kevin Leman

With Dad on a Deer Stand by Steve Chapman

TIME IN THE KITCHEN
RECIPES

Whole Wheat Yeast Rolls

2 envelopes rapid-rise active yeast

1¾ cups warm water

¼ cup sugar plus 2 tablespoons

2 teaspoons salt

½ cup butter, melted and divided

1 large egg, beaten

2¼ cups whole wheat flour

2¼ to 2½ cups all-purpose flour

Preheat oven to 400°F. Combine yeast, warm water, and 2 tablespoons sugar in a 2-cup liquid measuring cup, let stand for 5 minutes. Combine yeast mixture, remaining sugar, salt, ¼ cup melted butter, egg, and whole wheat flour in a large mixing bowl; beat on medium speed until well blended. Gradually add all-purpose flour to make soft dough. Turn dough out onto a well-floured surface; knead until smooth and elastic, approximately 5 to 10 minutes. Place in a well-greased bowl, turning to grease top. Cover and let rise in a warm place free from all drafts for 30 minutes or until doubled. Punch dough down, and divide in half; shape each into desired roll shape—crescent, cloverleaf, etc. Place in well-greased pan. Cover let rise in a warm place for approximately 20 minutes until doubled. Bake for 8 to 10 minutes until golden brown. Brush with remaining butter. Yields: 2 dozen.

Yeast Doughnuts

¼ cup warm water

2 tablespoons rapid-rise yeast

1½ cups warm milk

⅔ cup sugar

1¼ teaspoons salt

2 large eggs, beaten

⅓ cup shortening

5 cups all-purpose flour

In mixing bowl, whisk warm water and yeast together. Let stand 4 to 5 minutes making sure yeast is dissolved. Whisk in milk, sugar, salt, and eggs until blended. Add shortening and most of the flour, and blend. Knead dough with a dough hook on low speed until smooth; do not overmix. Remove dough from hook and coat with nonstick spray. Place back in bowl and cover bowl with clear plastic wrap. Let dough rise for 50 to 60 minutes until doubled. Turn dough onto floured surface and gently deflate. Roll to half-inch thickness and using a doughnut cutter, cut into doughnuts. Place on cookie sheet allowing room to rise. Cover loosely with plastic wrap and let rise 20 to 40 minutes. Heat oil in skillet to 350°F. Slide in doughnuts one at a time, frying 1 minute per side. Remove to wire rack set atop parchment paper. Cool.

TOP WITH GLAZE:

½ cup unsalted butter

1 ounce semisweet chocolate, melted

1½ teaspoons pure vanilla

2 cups confectioners' sugar

4 to 6 tablespoons hot water

Melt butter and chocolate on low heat. Remove and add vanilla and sugar. Stir in water as needed to desired thickness.

Sweet Cream Chocolate Cake

1 (4 ounce) unsweetened chocolate, melted

¾ cup unsalted butter

1½ cups sugar

3 large eggs, room temperature

2 egg yolks, room temperature

1 tablespoon pure vanilla

¼ cup strong coffee

1 cup whipping cream

½ cup ice water

2 cups all-purpose flour

¼ cup cocoa powder

2 teaspoons baking powder

1 teaspoon baking soda

½ teaspoon salt

Preheat oven to 325°F. Generously spray 2 (9-inch) pans and place on a parchment paper-lined baking sheet. Melt chocolate in microwave and allow to cool. In mixing bowl, cream butter and sugar until well blended. Fold in eggs, yolks, vanilla, and coffee. Blend well, 2 to 3 minutes, scraping bowl often to ensure nothing is stuck in well of mixer bowl. Blend in melted chocolate and then fold in whipping cream, water, flour, cocoa, baking powder, baking soda, and salt. Mix well on low speed until smooth. Pour batter into 9-inch prepared pans and bake for 45 to 50 minutes. Let cake cool on a rack in their pans.

Creamy Chocolate Icing

1 stick butter, softened

4 (1 ounce) squares chocolate, melted

3 teaspoons cocoa

2 teaspoons pure vanilla

⅓ cup half and half

4½ to 5 cups confectioners' sugar

In mixing bowl, cream butter, melted chocolate, and cocoa. Add vanilla and half & half. Gradually blend in confectioners' sugar to spreading consistency. Ice cooled cake.

Red Velvet Cupcakes

2¼ cups all-purpose flour

1 teaspoon salt

2 tablespoons red food color

3 tablespoons unsweetened cocoa

1 cup buttermilk

1 teaspoon vanilla

1½ cups sugar

1 stick butter, softened

2 eggs, room temperature

1 teaspoon baking soda

1 teaspoon white vinegar

Preheat oven to 350°F. Line standard muffin tin with paper baking cups. In mixing bowl, combine flour and salt. Gradually add food coloring into the cocoa in separate bowl until well blended. Set aside. Combine buttermilk and vanilla together in a small bowl. Beat sugar and butter with mixer until light and fluffy. Add eggs, one at a time, until creamy. Add cocoa mixture; beat well. Add flour mixture alternately with buttermilk mixture; beat until well blended. Combine baking soda and vinegar in small bowl and gently fold into batter with a spatula. Spoon batter into prepared muffin cups, fill two-thirds full. Bake 15 to 18 minutes or until toothpick inserted comes out clean. Cool on wire racks 10 minutes and remove from pan. Frost cupcakes with cream cheese icing; top with red sprinkles.

Cream Cheese Icing

1 stick butter (½ cup), room temperature

1 (8-ounce) package cream cheese, softened

1 tablespoon vanilla

6 to 8 cups powdered sugar

Cream butter and cream cheese until light and smooth. Add vanilla; mix well. Add powdered sugar one cup at a time until you reach the desired consistency. Pipe onto cupcakes and top with red sprinkles.

Heart-Shaped Cookies

5 cups all-purpose flour

2 cups sugar

1 teaspoon baking powder

¼ teaspoon baking soda

1 teaspoon salt

1 cup butter (2 sticks)

4 large eggs, room temperature

¼ cup milk

2 teaspoons vanilla

Preheat oven to 350°F. In large bowl, mix together flour, sugar, baking powder, baking soda, and salt. Cut in butter until mixture resembles coarse crumbs. Add eggs and mix well. Beat in milk and vanilla. Cover and chill at least 2 hours. Work with one-third of dough at a time on well-floured surface; roll dough to ¼-inch thick. Cut into heart shapes and place on lightly greased cookie sheet. Bake for 8 to 10 minutes, only until edges are the slightest brown. Cool 5 minutes; loosen cookies from cookie sheet. Ice cookies or dip in chocolate.

ICING:

2 cups powdered sugar, sifted

2 tablespoons butter, room temperature

¼ teaspoon almond extract (optional)

4 to 5 teaspoons milk

In a small bowl, beat together powdered sugar, butter, and almond extract with electric mixer. Beat in milk until icing is of piping consistency. For spreadable icing, add more milk. Red food coloring can be added if desired for heart shaped cookies.

DIPPING CHOCOLATE:

1 (12 ounce) package semisweet or milk chocolate chips

4 to 6 tablespoons oil

Pour chocolate chips in saucepan over low heat, or use a double boiler. Add oil and stir continually as chocolate melts. When melted, remove from heat and dip one side of each heart cookie; place on parchment or wax paper atop cookie sheet. Chill to set. <u>Note</u>: Ghirardelli® melting chocolates can be used in place of above recipe.

Spiced Hot Chocolate

2 cups milk

1 ounce semi-sweet chocolate

4 tablespoons cocoa powder

2 tablespoons warm water, approximately

¼ cup sugar

1 teaspoon ground cinnamon

½ teaspoon finely pulverized coffee granules

1 teaspoon cornstarch

½ teaspoon pure vanilla

2 pinches crushed red pepper flakes

In a 2-quart saucepan, heat milk over low heat. Melt chocolate in a small glass bowl in a microwave. Whisk cocoa, warm water, sugar, cinnamon, coffee granules, vanilla, and cornstarch into warm milk. Stir chocolate mixture into warmed milk. Stir in red pepper flakes. Heat until frothy. Pour into warmed-up glass mugs. Add marshmallows or top with fresh whipped cream.

Linda's Old Fashioned Sugar Cookie

1½ cups all-purpose flour, sifted

½ teaspoon baking powder

½ teaspoon salt

½ teaspoon baking soda

¾ cup sugar

½ cup shortening (if using butter, increase flour slightly)

1 egg, room temperature

2 heaping teaspoons milk

1 teaspoon vanilla

Preheat oven to 375°F. Sift together flour, baking powder, salt, soda, and sugar. Cut in shortening until mixture resembles coarse meal. Blend in egg, milk, and vanilla. Roll out on floured (use plenty!) board. Cut with cookie cutter; place on ungreased cookie sheets. Bake for about 6 to 8 minutes. <u>Note</u>: Ice if desired.

Peppermint Ice Cream

4 (7½ ounce) bags striped, round, hard peppermint candies

2 cups heavy cream

2 cups light cream, divided

In a blender or food processor bowl, place unwrapped candies and 1 cup light cream. Cover and blend or process until candies are crushed. Pour peppermint mixture into freezer can of an ice cream freezer. Stir in the remaining 1 cup light cream and heavy cream. Freeze according to manufacturer's directions. Makes 1½ quarts.

Strawberry Filled Cupcakes

2 cups all-purpose flour

2 ½ teaspoons baking powder

1 teaspoon salt

1 cup milk

2 teaspoons vanilla

1½ cups plus 3 tablespoons sugar, divided

½ cup butter, softened

3 eggs, room temperature

1½ cups whipping cream, cold

2 quarts fresh strawberries

Preheat oven to 350°F. Spray 18 standard muffin cups with nonstick spray. Combine flour, baking powder, and salt in medium bowl. Combine milk and vanilla in a small bowl. Beat 1½ cups sugar and butter in large bowl with mixer at medium speed until creamy. Add eggs one at a time. Add flour mixture alternately with milk mixture, beating until well blended. Spoon batter into greased muffin pan, ¾ full. Bake 15 to 18 minutes or until toothpick inserted comes out clean. Cool cupcakes on cooling rack 10 minutes. Remove from pans; cool completely on wire racks. Beat whipping cream in large bowl with electric mixer at high speed until soft peaks form. Gradually add remaining 3 tablespoons sugar; beat until stiff peaks form. Cut cupcakes in half crosswise. Place 2 tablespoons whipped cream and strawberries in the middle. Top with additional whipped cream and strawberries.

Lemon Bars

2½ cups all-purpose flour, divided

½ cup confectioners' sugar

¾ cup butter

½ teaspoon baking powder

4 large eggs, lightly beaten

2 cups sugar

1 teaspoon lemon rind, optional

⅓ cup lemon juice

Confectioners' sugar

Preheat oven to 350°F. In mixing bowl, combine 1½ cup flour and ½ cup confectioners' sugar; cut in the butter with fork or pastry blender until crumbly. Spoon mixture into a greased 9x13-inch pan; press firmly and evenly into bottom of pan. Bake for 20 minutes until lightly browned. Combine remaining 1 cup flour and baking powder. In separate bowl, combine eggs, 2 cups sugar, lemon rind, and lemon juice. Stir in flour mixture. Pour over prepared crust. Bake for 25 minutes until lightly brown and set. Cool and dust with confectioners' sugar.

Whole Wheat Orange Muffins

½ cup butter, melted

2 ¼ cups sugar

2 tablespoons honey

4 large eggs, room temperature

½ cup canola oil

1 cup buttermilk

1 teaspoon pure vanilla

½ teaspoon each lemon and orange extract

½ cup bran

5 cups all-purpose flour

¼ teaspoon baking soda

1 tablespoon baking powder

½ teaspoon salt

Preheat oven to 350°F. Line muffin pan with paper liners. Place on a baking sheet lined with parchment paper. Cream butter with sugar and honey. Add eggs and oil. Blend well. Stir in buttermilk, vanilla, flavorings, bran, and remaining ingredients making a soft batter. Using a cookie scoop, scoop batter into prepared muffin cups, filling until almost full. Bake for 25 to 30 minutes until done.

Sour Cream Blueberry Muffins

2¼ cups sugar

½ cup butter, melted

½ cup canola oil

4 large eggs, room temperature

1 teaspoon pure vanilla

4-5 cups all-purpose flour

¼ teaspoon baking soda

1 tablespoon baking powder

½ teaspoon salt

1 cup buttermilk

½ cup sour cream

2 cups blueberries

Sugar to dust tops

Preheat oven to 425°F. Place paper liners in muffin tin and place atop a parchment-lined cookie sheet. Blend sugar, butter, and oil. Whisk in eggs and vanilla. Fold into batter 4 cups flour, baking soda, baking powder, and salt. Mix well before blending in buttermilk and sour cream. Batter may be thin. If needed, add in additional flour. Gently fold in blueberries with spatula, try not to break berries apart turning the batter blue. Using cookie scoop, scoop a very large amount into prepared muffin cups, load as full as possible. Dust tops with sugar. Bake 15 minutes at 425°F then reduce temperature to 350°F and bake until golden brown, 12 to 16 minutes. Let cool.

Six-Ingredient Granola Bars

2 cups old-fashioned oatmeal

½ cup brown sugar

¾ cup raisins, dried cherries, or cranberries

½ cup raw honey

½ cup crunchy peanut butter/optional

1 stick butter, softened

Preheat oven to 350°F. Spray a 9x13 pan with nonstick cooking spray. Mix all ingredients in a large bowl. Press into prepared pan and bake for 15 to 18 minutes, until lightly brown. Cool for five minutes, cut into rectangles or squares, and cool completely before serving. Store in airtight container. Makes 18 bars. Note: Peanut butter, almond butter, or butter can be used interchangeably.

Christine's Fabulous Coconut Smoothie

1 cup coconut milk, chilled

1 scoop high-quality protein powder

2 tablespoons ground flax seed meal

1 large banana

1 teaspoon coconut flavoring

10 ice cubes

Combine all the above ingredients in a blender and puree until smooth. Top with toasted, unsweetened coconut. For other fruit flavors, simply replace the coconut with peaches, mango, strawberries, or blueberries.

Peanut Butter Coconut Power Balls

1 cup dry old-fashioned oatmeal

1 cup Toasted Coconut, lightly toasted

½ cup natural peanut butter

¼ cup ground flax seed

¼ cup wheat germ

½ cup dark chocolate chips

¼ cup raw honey

1 teaspoon pure vanilla

Mix together all ingredients in a large mixing bowl until well blended. Chill for 1 hour. Once chilled, roll into balls the desired size and place on cookie sheet; chill 30 minutes. Store in an airtight container for up to 1 week. Makes 20 to 25 balls. Ground flax seed and wheat germ can be found in the cereal/health food sections of the local grocery.

Toasting Coconut: Preheat oven at 350°F. Spread coconut evenly onto large cookie sheet. Bake for 10 minutes and then remove from oven. Using a fork, stir coconut and place back in oven for 5 more minutes until golden brown. Cool and store in zipper bag until needed.

Whole Wheat Pita Chips

10 whole-wheat pita rounds, cut into wedges
1½ tablespoons olive oil
1½ teaspoons paprika
1½ tablespoons dried oregano

Preheat oven to 400°F. Toss pita wedges with oil, paprika, and oregano in large bowl. Spread on a baking sheet and bake until golden brown, about 20 to 25 minutes. Store in airtight container.

Cheesy Almond Spread

1 (8 ounce) package cream cheese, softened
1½ cups (6 ounce) Swiss cheese, shredded
½ cup almonds, sliced
⅓ cup mayonnaise
2 green onions, chopped
¼ teaspoon ground nutmeg
¼ teaspoon pepper
Garnish: Almond slices, toasted

Preheat oven to 350°F. Combine first 7 ingredients, stir well. Spread mixture into a 9-inch pie plate. Bake uncovered for 15 minutes until bubbly. Garnish with almond slices. Serve with pita chips.

Pan-Seared Cod

½ cup panko bread crumbs
½ cup pecans, finely chopped
⅓ cup flour
1 teaspoon baking powder
1 teaspoon salt
1 teaspoon black pepper
1 teaspoon paprika
½ cup buttermilk
1½ pounds Cod fillets
4 tablespoons butter
1 lemon, cut in wedges for serving

In shallow dish, combine panko crumbs and pecans. In another dish, combine flour, baking powder, salt, pepper, and paprika. In a third dish, add buttermilk. Taking one filet at a time, dust in flour mixture and shake off excess. Dip filet in buttermilk to evenly coat, drain excess. Dredge in pecan mixture, coating thoroughly. In a large skillet, heat butter over medium heat; and cook on each side for 2-3 minutes, or until fish is golden, flakes with a fork and reaches a safe internal temperature of 145°F. Serve with fresh lemon wedges, refrigerate any leftovers.

Creamy Salmon Fillets

¼ cup shallots

2 tablespoons butter, melted

½ cup white wine vinegar

½ cup water

4 Salmon fillets

Sea salt and pepper to taste

½ cup heavy cream

3 tablespoons fresh parsley, chopped

In skillet with lid over medium heat, heat shallots in butter, white wine vinegar, and water for 3-4 minutes. Season salmon with salt and pepper. Place atop shallots, cover and cook over low heat for 10 minutes, turning after 5 minutes. Cook to desired texture. Remove and keep warm. Add heavy cream to skillet; stir and cook over high heat until reduced by half. Add chopped parsley and pour over salmon fillets. Serve warm.

Trout Amandine

3 tablespoons butter

¼ cup sliced almonds

½ cup milk

1 egg yolk

½ teaspoon hot sauce

1 cup all-purpose flour

1 teaspoon salt

1 teaspoon pepper

6 (12 ounce) Rainbow Trout fillets

Olive oil

Lemon Cream Sauce

Melt butter in a large skillet over low heat. Add almonds and sauté until golden brown. Remove almonds from skillet and drain on paper towels. Set aside. In small bowl, whisk together milk, egg yolk, and hot sauce. In additional bowl, stir together flour, salt, and pepper. Dredge fillets in flour mixture; dip in egg mixture. Dredge an additional time in the flour mixture. Pour oil in skillet; heat to 375°F. Cook fillets 3 to 4 minutes on each side until golden brown. Spoon Lemon Cream sauce over each fillet and top with sautéed almonds.

LEMON CREAM SAUCE:

½ cup butter

2 tablespoons flour

1 (14½ ounce) can chicken broth

2 garlic cloves, minced

1 tablespoon lemon juice

⅓ cup whipping cream

¼ cup white wine Worchester sauce

½ teaspoon salt

½ teaspoon hot sauce

Over medium heat melt butter in skillet; whisk in flour. Cook and whisk for one minute. Add broth, garlic, lemon juice; whisk and bring to a boil. Reduce heat and simmer, whisking constantly for approximately five minutes. Whisk in cream and remaining ingredients, and cook for additional five minutes until thick.

WORKBOOK REFERENCE LIST

Alvanti, Christine. *Skinny Chicks Eat Real Food.* (Emmaus, Rodale Publishing, 2012), 147–148.

Blankenship, Sherry. *Draw Near.* (Tate Publishing, 2007). 199.

Chappa, Deborah R. *Words for When There Are no Words: Writing a Memorable Condolence Note* (Haverford, Infinity Publishing, 1999).

Elliot, Elisabeth. *A Chance to Die.* (Revell Publishing, 1987).

Ewer, Cynthia. "Pantry Recipes for Homemade Cleaning Products." *www.organized.com/recipesforhomemadecleaningproducts.com*

Felton, Sandra. *The Messies Manual* (Revell Publisher Grand Rapids, Michigan 2005).

Halvorson, Christine. *Arm & Hammer Baking Soda, Over 100 Helpful Household Hints.* 1998. Lincolnwood: Publishers International, Ltd.

Home Furnishings. "Room arrangements," *www.homefurnish.com/livingroomdecor/homedecor/roomarrangements.aspx*

How to Beat House-work. Lincolnwood: Eureka Vacuum Cleaners Publication International, Ltd. 1988. Lansky, Vicki.

Baking Soda: Over 500 Fabulous, Fun, and Frugal Uses You've Probably Never Thought Of. 2004. Minnetonka: Book Peddlers.

McNulty, JoAnne. "Age Appropriate Chores for Kids." *www.freeprintablebehaviorcharts.com.*

Mitchell, Nancy R. "Etiquette Rules!." 2017. New York, New York: Well Fleet Press.

Paper, Heather J. *Home Decorating* (Taunton Press, 2005).

The Taste of Home Cookbook (Reiman Media Group Inc. 2009).

West, Kay. *How to Raise a Gentleman—A Civilized Guide to Helping Your Son Through His Uncivilized Childhood.* 2001. Nashville: Rutledge Hill Press-Division of Thomas Nelson Publishers, Inc.

West, Kay. *How to Raise a Lady—A Civilized Guide to Helping Your Daughter Through Her Uncivilized Childhood.* 2001. Nashville: Rutledge Hill Press-Division of Thomas Nelson Publishers, Inc.

Wimmer Cookbooks. *Why Didn't I Think of That?* 1993. Memphis: Wimmer Cookbooks.

About

THE AUTHOR

Dianne Dougharty was married to her high school sweetheart for forty-five years. After an extended illness, Mark went to be with Jesus on July 31, 2018. She is the mother of two daughters and Mimi to seven grandchildren. Dianne graduated from Trevecca Nazarene University with a degree in Elementary Education. For over thirty years, she has led women's Bible studies, spoken at conferences, authored curriculum, and contributed written work to several blogs. She faithfully served for years beside her husband in full-time vocational ministry.

Dianne has a desire to see older women fulfill the mandate given them in Titus 2:3-4, "These older women must train the younger women to love their husbands and their children, to live wisely and be pure, to work in their homes, to do good, and to be submissive to their husbands. Then they will not bring shame to the word of God." NLT

Her heart is for young women to become seekers of Christ, students of God's Word, and lovers of their home, husband, family, and calling. She has a passion to see women live purposefully—making investments in the lives of other women.

God led Dianne to develop the Secrets Savored Ministry, a fun hands-on approach to developing community among women who desire to create a spirit of hospitality and Christlikeness within their lives, homes, and relationships—for the glory of God! Once a week, small groups meet within home settings and learn to apply biblical principles for living a godly life in an often God-less world.

Check out the ministry at secretssavored.org.

CONNECT WITH HER ON FACEBOOK & INSTAGRAM @SECRETSSAVORED

Secrets Savored
PARTICIPATION INFO SHEET

NAME: _____

SINGLE: _____

MARRIED: 1–5 years _____ 6–10 years _____ More than 10 years _____

AGE: 15–22 _____ 23–30 _____ 31–35 _____ over 35 _____

E-MAIL: _____

ADDRESS: _____

_____

_____

CELL PHONE: _____

WORK PHONE: _____

ALLERGIES: _____

Tell us about yourself. For Example: Where did you go to school? Where do you work? Where did you grow up? Do you have any unusual life experiences? Do you have any children? If so, how many and what are their ages

SECRETS *Savored*

CREATING COMMUNITY THROUGH SIMPLE HOSPITALITY

Secrets Savored is a Titus 2 discipling tool. Women across generations discover the treasure of community as they practice simple hospitality and apply Biblical truths in a home setting. This in-depth Bible study is growing women into a deeper faith and building Christ-like character within them.

CONNECT WITH US @SECRETSSAVORED

Books are available for purchase as eBook. Visit secretssavored.org to order.

Made in United States
Cleveland, OH
18 December 2024